Energy and the Future of Humanity

Energy and the Future of Humanity

by

Alex Markman

ASTEROID
PUBLISHING Inc

Energy and the Future of Humanity

Asteroid Publishing, Inc.

ISBN-13: 978-1530990795
ISBN-10: 1530990793

Contents

Introduction

Humans are the only species of all animal kingdom who are concerned about the future. In fact, on individual level our perception of it is the foundation of our most important decisions: choice of profession, marriage, plans for retirements, and so on.

For social units, from families to small communities, to multinational corporations and to the governments the future planning and forecast is a component of their modern primary activities and responsibilities.

No matter how good and thorough our plans and their executions might be, reality invariably confronts us with the unexpected – in most cases not in our favour.

Is there a way to know what we do right or wrong, as individuals or as a community, or as a society? In the passing moment of action it is almost impossible to judge that with any degree of accuracy. If we could, we would always do right things and make right decisions. Obviously, this is not the case.

When someone goes to work, they assume that it would take as much time to get there as it was in the past. But accidents happen, and the short-term plan falls apart. When someone plans for retirement, he/she assumes living long enough to enjoy the golden age. But terminal illness may happen, or accident, or break of the family, or any other unpredictable event, which makes all planning and forecast obsolete.

People always knew how unpredictable the human destiny is, and therefore how futile an attempt to peek into it. To satisfy their curiosity, all kind of fortune tellers emerged, along with pseudo-sciences such as numerology, astrology, and the likes.

However, predicting the future of a society is a different matter: it can be based on precedents, history, and detectable technological and social trends.

The only guide to evaluate our actions is a common sense of the passing moment and to look back at history and learn from our past mistakes. However, the same history tells us that no matter how sophisticated a society is, it invariably goes through wars, crises and turmoil.

Prognosis of the future became vital for the global politics of all countries, regardless of their size and power. Some countries develop faster than others, and become, quite unexpectedly, big players in geopolitical game. Others deteriorate, also contrary to expectations of others. Alliances change accordingly: with them emerge new security and economic challenges for all. Predicting these challenges is the best knowledge a country could acquire to prepare itself to face the transforming reality.

The larger an entity, and the longer the stretch of time is, the more accurate a prediction could be. In the second half of the twentieth century the future forecasts became a discipline of social science. International conglomerates do it routinely every year, either themselves of hiring specialised consulting agencies. And so do the governments.

In spite of all accumulated expertise, no forecast is accurate. Particularly in the modern times, when social and technological dynamics accelerate, something unexpected comes about, forcing societies to re-evaluate their prognosis and actions.

This book is about the future circa 2030, and beyond. In the following analysis, the guess work was removed as much as possible. Facts, recognized trends, and logical arguments are the primary instruments in forecasting technique in this monograph.

Chapter 1. Unpredictable shocks in the past and in the future.

Is it possible to predict the future without much speculation and guesswork? How reliable the forecast could be without them? After all, even in not so distant past there had been a few turning points in modern history, which no one was able to predict, or support their prediction with a meaningful evidence and logic. Among many, there were three most profound ones, which shaped the contemporary world politics.

In 1979, the Iranian revolution ended the Shah's rule. Some among Western politicians and analysts expressed a warm welcome to the new regime. The argument was that this was a positive change, a liberation from the oppressive Shah's regime, and expression of the nation's free will. It turned out to be a regime of religious fanatics. Its impact on international affairs was enormous. It started the era of militant Islam assault on the Western world and a large scale international terrorism. The contemporary turmoil in the Middle East, and hostility among different factions of Islam and different nationalities in this region are in most part the result of Islamic revolution in Iran, and its support to terrorist and radical Muslim groups around the world. Iran's agenda has been clearly expressed by its leadership time and again: war on infidels of all kinds. Among them, America and Israel are the primary targets. Before the revolution, all these 'enemies' cooperated with Iran, and contributed to its economy and cooperated in technological progress. Only a few analysts, if any, had been able to predict its

5

fanatical hostility towards the countries of Western culture. It did not make sense for the Western mentality. But it is different in Iran. Islamic radicalism found a fertile ground not only in Iran, but in all Muslim countries in the region.

In 1980, the China phenomenon had begun. When Chinese government started its reforms, no one predicted that in less than 30 years this country would become the second economy in the world after the United States. Its development progressed with no violence, very little internal turmoil, and no political blackmail or threat to its neighbours or the Western World.

In predictions of China's future, mostly sceptics had prevailed, and rightly so. The communist system by nature of its power and ideology is hostile to the capitalist system and the free enterprise. As a matter of fact, it is hostile to any freedom, economical or not, and therefore could only be detrimental to economy development. There is no communist country in the world, former or in existence, which had reached prosperity. After collapse of the Soviet Union, all its republics plunged into appalling poverty and criminal chaos. The countries of the former Eastern Block, eager to adapt to capitalist system, did not fair better. They still struggle to reach the Western level of efficiency, but so far with a very modest success.

The most impressive example of the Communist system legacy is East Germany. Its population is still not 100% integrated with West Germany. And this is one nation, one country, which was split just for 45 years!

Thirty years later, defying all forecasts and fossilised notions of Communist rule, China had become the second world economy and military power. Its contribution to development of new products, machinery and even technology is tremendous. Thanks to its cheap labour, prototype manufacture becomes very affordable not only for corporations, but also for private inventors and entrepreneurs. In many instances affordability of Chinese labour contributed to rise of modern industries. The case in point is panels and elements for solar energy generation, imported from China to the US. If not for low prices, this industry would not have reached the existing mass production in such short period of time. But once the industry reaches the critical mass, it grows like a snow ball: the bigger it gets, the faster it grows.

In 1991 the world witnessed a spectacular collapse of the Soviet Union. It was accompanied by stream of shocking news and revelations. Its disintegration was followed by dissolution of all communist parties in Europe, and in the most parts of the globe.

Collapse of the Soviet Union affected not only the life of its former republics, but in a more profound way the global politics. It ended the confrontation of two superpowers - the United States and the Soviet Union - and terminated their respective controls over geopolitical areas, which they inherited after the WWII.

The consensus among politicians and analysts was that the new era has began for the countries of the Eastern block. This supposed to be the era of democracy and prosperity for the these countries, and their future integration into the community of Western societies. The reality turned out to be not that rosy.

Living conditions of all Eastern block countries got worse. In most of the former Soviet Union republics dictatorship was established: exception were only Baltic republics. Russia and Ukraine governance was far from being democratic: these were half-dictatorial regimes, with widespread corruption, limited freedom of economic activity and suppressed opposition. In the following 25 years both Russia and Ukraine demonstrated their inability to develop a minimal self-sustained economy and working democratic institutions. East European countries show a better progress, but they still struggle in tenets of economic problems.

Russia's international policy may seem puzzling to the Western mentality. This country's well-being is dependent on oil and gas trade with Western Europe. In no lesser extent it depends on foreign investment in its industrial infrastructure, and its technology. Under such circumstances it is logical to suggest that the country would be interested in maintaining good relations with Western Europe, and possibly even some integration with it. But the reality is opposite: Russia, as Iran, declared all democratic countries as its enemies, became hostile towards its neighbours, and became a friend to the most oppressive regimes, such as North Korea, Iran and Syria. This policy is accompanied by shrinking economy and worsening of population's living conditions. Nonetheless, most of the Russian population supports this policy. Does it make sense? Could any analyst with Western mentality predict it?

The cornerstone of all predictions - or projections - is our perception of reality. Our understanding of probability in its intuitive form is that the future is going to be a variation of the present. There are times that this thinking is right. But there are other times, when forces, growing within societies, invisible for the most, become unruly monsters, and bring about drastic changes.

In life of all societies there are hidden forces at work. They usually gather strength slowly, but at certain, unpredictable point in time their intensity gathers speed exponentially, and eventually erupt as a volcano.

It is impossible to predict behaviour of governments and individual societies in different circumstances. As history demonstrates, irrational decision of one player triggers the chain reaction of other players, and then it is hard to make a rational decision from an irrational one.

The undercurrents of change bring about different results in different societies. Thus, Japan, with its leading military caste, morphed into powerful, but peaceful economy after the WWII. China, ruled by one of the most oppressive communist regimes under Mao, became the second powerful economy in the world. Israel, established on a small piece of non-liveable land, became one of the most technologically advanced countries in the world. But at the same token, Russia, the richest country in the world in terms of land and resources, became one of the poorest countries in Euro-Asia continent, with semi-dictatorial regime. Middle East countries are in tenets of sectarian and ethnical hostility, and live in poverty in spite of enormous donations from the rich Arab countries and the UN. Is there any common undercurrent, which may bring about global changes to all?

There is one, which is quite obvious: accelerated progress and amalgamation of science and technology.

Until the beginning of twentieth century, scientific discoveries and technological innovations were achievements of individual brilliant minds, fascinated by mystery of nature and power of technology. They lived, and worked on meagre donations of governments, individuals and corporations. After the WWI, both science and technology progress became the matter of collective mind: laboratories, design entities and experiments became a part of huge network, which included universities, corporations, and governments. Still the role of geniuses is great, but their work is in the framework of a huge system, whose collective mind is thousands of times greater than it was in the whole preceding history of humanity. Now, both governments and corporations set up goals and draft the desired results, which they expect to get from scientific and technological organizations.

Today, in the middle of the first decade of 21st century, we witness the immediate impact of two major developments; progress in information technology and advancement in the field of energy generation. The last one manifests itself in sharp drop of oil prices, accompanied by increased energy consumption. Other technologies are coming into play, and bring with them changes even more profound than any we have witnessed so far. Their accelerated progress inevitably will trigger social and political changes. What are they? What will happen if the energy will be in abundance?

The first thought that comes to mind is that it will be a golden age for humanity: indefinite expansion of economy, high living standard for all, elimination of poverty, and cure of most of social ills. Science and technology will continue its spectacular progress, which will ensure physical and mental health of population, provision of high quality social services, and reduced social and political tensions around the globe. Unfortunately, it will never happen even under the ideal circumstances. In every positive trend, be it pure social, or technological, or both, there are seeds of decay or destruction. For instance, abundance of food in America caused obesity epidemics, for which no cure yet has been found. Availability of social assistance in rich societies resulted in unprecedented number of welfare recipients. In the recent past, a well-developed democracy in Germany paved the way for Nazi regime, which was supported by majority of population. Technological progress in 19th and 20th centuries brought humanity to two world wars, which casualties and destruction were the greatest in the human history. There is no need to provide more examples. Suffice it to say that there is no exception: the greater is the force – and effect – of any trend, be it positive or negative, the more powerful becomes the force of its destruction. We will discuss this issue in the following chapters of this work.

Chapter 2. Energy generation trends.

Energy is the fuel of economy. During the course of industrial revolution, and up to the second half of the twentieth century, its sources were in abundance, and comparatively easy to access. But since late 1960 its production began lagging behind the demand, thereby negatively affecting global economy, and causing military and political tensions in the locales of oil extraction.

Even the ignorant already understand how explosive, and potentially disastrous energy problem may become in the near future. Most of fossil fuel discoveries are in the politically unstable parts of the globe. This factor alone puts in jeopardy the economy of Western Europe, and to some extent the US. Constantly increasing demand for oil and gas may outpace its new exploration and production.

Developing world fairs no better: China and India, and other quickly developing economies could push the oil price to new heights. And last, not the least, is the disastrous impact of fossil fuel burning on the environment. It is not about the global warming: let scientists discuss it in depth whether it is caused by human activity or not. The issue under consideration is poisonous pollution, causing epidemic of various, in the past rare, diseases such as skeletal structure deterioration, mental disorders, and many others, for which no effective cure has been found yet.

Progress of traditional energy technologies, along with emerging ones, has already triggered processes which will change in the near future the life of humanity beyond any fantasy. Even more profound, and largely unexpected consequences of technological advancement will take place in the next 70-100 years. The seeds of changes are already detectable. It is just the matter of understanding their significance, and using statistics and already traceable dynamics to deduce their outcome in the future.

The major social-economic engine in the contemporary political and economical life on the global scale is energy generating technology. In the last 50 years we witnessed a vivid demonstration of its impact on global economies and politics. Arab countries, which did not have any meaningful economy and military power, but had large reserves of oil and gas, imposed their rules of political game on the whole world. They dictated oil prices at will, without any relation to the cost of its extraction and distribution cost. For example, the extraction cost of Saudi Arabian oil is $4-$5 US. At its peak the oil price was almost $140. Supply and demand imbalance is too shallow and explanation. The root of the problem is that the known oil reserves were mostly under control of a few oil producing countries, and no meaningful alternative to the existing oil supply was available up to the recent past.

Energy cost, and the cost of its major component - oil, have been a strong impediment to economy growth elsewhere. As soon as business activity picked up, the demand for energy grew, and with it grew the price of oil. The higher the oil price hiked, the stronger was its negative impact on economy growth.

There is nothing new in this observation, however it is important to mention these facts for understanding the latest development in energy generation technology, and the reason of contemporary impressive 2014 oil price drop. The Chart 1 below shows the price of oil in the last 15 years.

Chart 1. Recent History of Oil Price

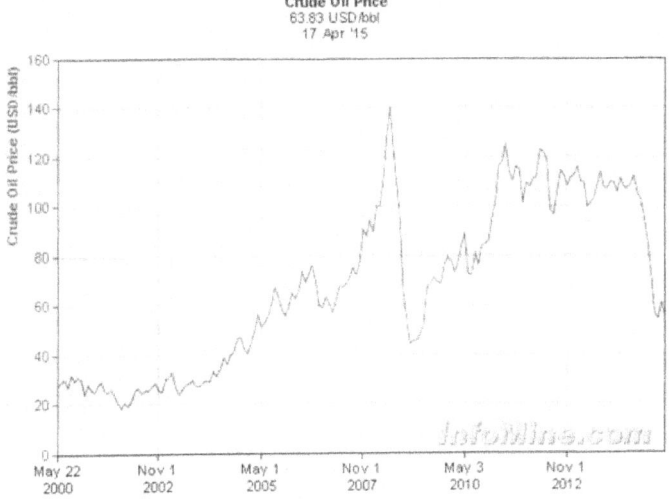

Fifteen years ago the price of oil was close to $25.00 per barrel. As energy consumption grew around the globe, and particularly so in the US and China, the price of oil climbed steadily to $132.00 per barrel in 2008. Then the economic crisis hit the U.S., and spread over the world. Understandably, the price of oil dropped in accordance with demand. The cause and affect is straightforward here, and does not require much understanding of the relation between economic factors.

After this price drop, the global and the U.S. economy began its steady recovery. The price of oil climbed with it, but fail to reach the previous peak. Some gurus predicted then that the price of oil will reach $200.00 for a barrel, if not more. But in 2014, defying the previous patterns, the world economy continued to grow, but the price of oil began its steep descent, diving below

$50 per barrel in January 2015. The big question is: was it just a temporary blip in mechanisms of economy, or a logical outcome of the events, which would stay permanently with us in the near future, thus keeping the price of oil at the contemporary level, or even lower?

In order to identify the trends of the future, it is necessary to understand why the oil price dropped. There have been a few developments, which produced their combined effect on oil and gas demand. Some of them are of temporary nature, whereas other will remain in effect in many decades to come. Statistics below sheds light at the issue.

The world production figures, presented by BP in its annual report in 2014, give us very interesting information (Table 1).

Table 1. World Oil Production

Year	2008	2009	2010	2011	2012	2013
1,000s b/ Day	82,955	81,262	82,296	84,049	86,204	86,754

Supply and demand logic suggests that oil consumption should grow in step with oil production. However, the Table 2 shows different picture.

Table 2. Total World Oil Consumption.

Year	2008	2009	2010	2011	2012	2013
1,000s b/day	86,147	85,111	87,801	88,934	89,931	91,331

As tables 1 and 2 demonstrate, the oil production growth is slower than the pace of world consumption. Therefore, according to supply and demand relation, the price of oil should rise accordingly, but the opposite occurred.

As the BP report explains, "Differences between world consumption figure and world production statistics are accounted for by stock changes, consumption of non-petroleum additives and substitute fuels." And, even more to the point, "Consumption of biogasoline (such as ethanol), biodiesel and derivatives of coal and natural gas are also included."

This is what has been happening in the last few years. Consumption of energy increases faster than production of oil, however alternative sources of energy came into play, such as biodisel, biogasoline, and others. But there are other developments, which affect oil price now, and will in the future.

I will group them into two categories: Transient and Permanent.

The Transient category combines factors and technological improvements of fossil fuel extraction and exploration, as well as production of its substitutions, such as biofuel or other liquefied products.

Permanent category comprises new technology trends, which will remain in force in the foreseeable future. The most important ones are renewable sources of energy, and coming of age fuel cell technology. There is a very promising progress in nuclear technology, but it is outside the scope of this analysis.

The Worldwatch institute considers the following types renewable energy: Solar, Wind, biofuels, Hydro. In its report of April 10, 2015 it stated: "...today so much has happened in the renewable energy sector during the past five years that our perceptions lag far behind the reality of where the industry is today."

BP Energy Outlook 2035 report goes even further: Renewables are expected to continue to be the fastest growing class of energy, gaining market share from a small base as they rise at an average of 6.4% a year to

2035. Renewables' share of global electricity production is expected to grow from 5% to 14% by 2035.

In 2013, renewable electrical global capacity was, as shown in the table 3 below (not counting hydro power).

Table 3. Renewable Electricity Global Capacity (1)

Technology	GW*
Bio-power	88
Geothermal power	12
Ocean power	0.5
Solar PV	139
Concentrating solar thermal power	3.4
Wind power	318
Total	560

*GW – Gigawatt = 1,000 megawatt.

Developments in the early 2000s showed upwards trends in global renewable energy investment, and integration across all sectors. Yet most mainstream projections did not predict the extraordinary expansion of renewables that was to unfold over the decade ahead. Scenarios from the renewable energy industry experts, from the International Energy Agency, the World Bank, Greenpeace, and others, all projected levels of renewable energy for the year 2020 that had already been exceeded by 2010.

In the following discussion nuclear and hydropower are not considered, as their expansion, with the use of existing technology, is problematic. Thus, as stated in Solar FAQ's, an average nuclear power plant operates at average capacity of 1 GW. "Hence, to produce 15 TW (15,000 GW) by 2050 would require roughly 14,636 new 1-GW nuclear power plants. Construction of this number of plants would require, on average, the commissioning of a new nuclear power plant somewhere in the world every day continuously for 40 years."

This scale of construction is not feasible even if there is intention and determination of all nations to do so. First, funds required for such construction are too big even for the whole humanity. Second, it is not probability, but rather a certainty that major disasters will happen on a regular basis. And last, but not the least: the same source informs that "...the estimated global conventional uranium terrestrial resources would be exhausted in less than 10 years."

These considerations are valid only under assumption that the contemporary technology remains the basis for new plants. A major break through in nuclear applied science may change the situation. The risk associated with nuclear power will always be present though, particularly with significant increase in numbers of operating plants.

Hydropower, although significant, has much smaller potential than wind and solar sources. Its negative impact on environment is also significant in most locations, and its up-front capital expense is too large, impeding proliferation of this technology.

Another factor affecting oil price came into play with proliferation of shale oil production in the U.S. It belongs to the Transient category, as it is of temporary nature: its use is defined by market forces, environmental considerations, and technological improvements. Its production is expensive, but when the price on international market rises above its production cost, this method of oil extraction gathers steam.

In a very short period of time this technology improved considerably. With its expansion, further improvements have been made, which reduced production cost and environmental impact. However, its further use

Chapter 3. Solar energy generation.

Simply put, solar energy is the energy from the sun. It is available, in different intensity, to all countries around the globe. It is plentiful and free, the gift of God, so to speak. As stated in Wikipedia "The amount of solar energy reaching the surface of the planet is so vast that in one year it is about twice as much as will ever be obtained from all of the Earth's non-renewable resources of coal, oil, natural gas, and mined uranium combined."

Actually, scientists had calculated the theoretical potential of using solar energy hitting the earth. It is 89,300 TW (although estimates varies). Compare it to the contemporary total world consumption of 15 TW: it is approximately 6,000 times more then all sources we currently use for energy generation.

In practical terms, not all this energy is available for harvesting. It is spread over all earth's surface, but its collection is limited to small areas where conversion panels are installed. The amount of energy received by these locations is limited to average 6-7 hours a day, but could be less or more, depending on weather conditions, season, and latitude. When it is located at considerable distance from consumers, which is often the case, the electricity transmission infrastructure has to be built to deliver electricity to its destination. As the solar energy is not evenly spread over time of day, some mechanism must be created to store generated electricity for later use.

The greater is the solar energy conversion facility, the larger land area must be used, which also may be a problem in densely populated areas. However, when efficiency of solar technology improves, considerably less surface is required to generate the same amount of energy.

Advantages of solar energy are obvious:
- Amount of solar energy far exceeds any other sources known to humanity
- There is virtually zero pollution in converting the solar energy into electricity or other form of energy
- It may reduce demand for fossil fuels to a small fraction of what it is now, thus profoundly diminishing pollution and dependence on fossil fuel supply
- When cost of a kilowatt production from solar energy drops below the cost of fossil fuels, this source of energy will affect the price of fossil fuels and the cost of goods production

The idea of harvesting solar energy is not new. However, the cost of producing electricity from it had been prohibitively high up until 21st century. According to IEA, when the PV (photovoltaic) technology was first developed in 1950s, the price of solar PV cells was $300 per watt. It took more than 25 years to reduce the price of a cell to $76.00 in 1977. Since then, the price began a spectacular march down with increased velocity. In 2012 the price was 0.97 per watt. It seemed to experts that this was close to the theoretical limit. They were wrong. The cost was decreasing even in faster pace. The Chart 2 below demonstrates its dynamics since 1977.

Chart 2. Price history of silicon PV cells

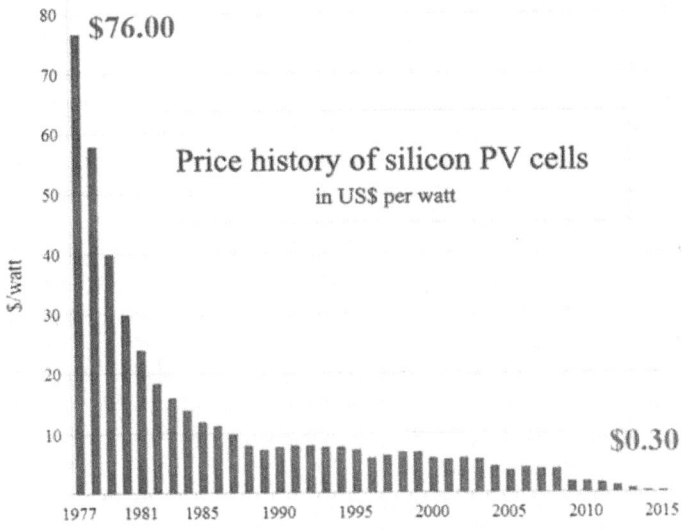

Now, the price per watt in 2015 is expected to be $0.30, three times less than just 3 years ago! Is it close to the limit? Far from it. The industry is still in its infancy, as we will see in the following discussion. Until 2013, the solar PV global capacity have grown exponentially, as shown in Table 4.

Table 4. Solar PV Global Capacity (5)

Year	Gigawatts
2004	3.7
2005	5.1
2006	7
2007	9
2008	16
2009	23
2010	40
2011	70
2012	100
2013	139

So far, the solar energy industry have grown with maximum PV solar panels efficiency 15%. Even with this constrain, in 2015 the world solar energy generation exceeded 200 terawatt hours (TWh) of electricity per year. Estimated generation in 2020 is close to 500 TWh. The Table 5 below shows impressive rise of PV solar energy use.

Table 5. Global generation of solar electricity (6)

Electricity Generation from Solar		
Year	Energy (TWh)	% of Total
2004	2.6	0.01%
2005	3.7	0.02%
2006	5.0	0.03%
2007	6.8	0.03%
2008	11.4	0.06%
2009	19.3	0.10%
2010	31.4	0.15%
2011	60.6	0.27%
2012	96.7	0.43%
2013	134.5	0.58%
2014	185.9	0.79%
Source: BP-Statistical Review of World Energy, 2015		

The interesting phenomena is, that the price of PV cells, and meteoric growth of the solar generating industry so far had little to do with efficiency. Usually, the more efficient the process is, the less expensive its output. But with PV cells, the price was influenced by a few other factors. Which one had more weight than others is hard to determine; most likely all forces worked in sync. They are:

1. Public opinion, demanding cleaner energy generation process, as harm to the environment and ecologic health threatens the whole life on earth. Respectively, the policy of incentives was introduced in some countries to the industries of renewable energy.
2. Improvement in manufacturing process of PV cells, which affected the cost of production
3. Economy of scale: as soon as production reached the critical mass, the price per unit began its slide down
4. China factor: China produced PV panels for such a low price that the technology became affordable to many private companies and countries around the globe. The largest buyer of them was the U.S.
5. The high price of oil, which made the energy cost of solar generators competitive with fossil fuel cost.

In 2014 the price of oil suddenly dropped. I use the word 'suddenly' because no serious analyst predicted such drop and at that particular time. After all, oil price fluctuation is not a new phenomenon. This had happened many times in the past. However, this time the low price might stay for long, as different technologies, renewables among them, come into play. The cost of electricity produced by renewables became competitive with fossil fuel energy. Comparative cost of electricity produced by different technologies in 2014 is shown in table 6.

Table 6. Levelized * cost of electricity produced by different technologies. (7)

Power Plant Type	Cost $/kW-hr
Coal	$0.10-0.14
Natural Gas	$0.07-0.13
Nuclear	$0.10
Wind	$0.08-0.20
Solar PV	$0.13
Solar Thermal	$0.24
Geothermal	$0.05
Biomass	$0.10
Hydro	$0.08

*levelized cost = the average total cost to build and operate a power-generating asset over that time.

There had been a few projections into the future of solar energy, but they became outdated at the time of their publication. Whatever happened in R&D in the field of solar PV efficiency between 2013 and 2015 made statistical-mathematical models, used so far, inadequate. None of them predicted technological breakthroughs, resulting in much higher energy efficiency of PV cells.
Energy efficiency is the percentage of sunlight hitting a panel and getting turned into electricity for practical use. The notion of its theoretical limit was being changed from one height to another. Thus, in 2013 reports, the maximum efficiency of solar panels believed to be 15%. And up until that point in time, most installations had just that. However, recently the latest commercial module

efficiency reached 25.6%. No sooner as it was announced, another news stunned the gurus: "In December 2014, a solar cell achieved a new laboratory record with 46% efficiency in a French-German collaboration." (8)

As commercial production of these panels approaches, further research reached new heights. Universities and a few private companies are close to achieve 95% efficiency of solar cells. They use Pentacene, an organic material, which is naturally present in green leaves. This is an organic semiconductor: with the same quantity of light it doubles the energy capacity of the most efficient known non-organic semiconductor. Research is under way to use other organic or combination of organic and non-organic substances, which promise to achieve the same 95% efficiency.

This information is already sufficient to make projection into the future of PV solar industry. In 2013, the total investment in 15% efficiency industry in the world was $112 bill, as shown in the Table 7.

Table 7. Global New Investment in Renewable Energy by Technology, Billion $

Technology	Developed	Developing	total
Solar	74.8	38.9	113.7
Wind	36.0	44.0	80

In further analysis we assume that the amount of investment will remain the same till the year 2030. How realistic is this assumption? Actually, the evidence is that it can only increase, and substantially at that. As of 2014, the cost of kWt/hr of PV solar electricity generators was $0.13. With efficiency of 46% the expected cost is three times less, roughly about $0.05 kWt/hr. With efficiency of 70%, the expected price is $0.03 kWt/hr. This is the cheapest energy that ever existed: less expensive than coal, gas, or even wind generated electricity. No doubt that increased investment will flow into this technology with accelerated pace. However, the more efficient the PV unit gets, the less investment is required for the same amount of electricity. That is why the conservative estimate is adopted.

Along with improved efficiency, other factors will accelerate solar technology proliferation:

- Public opinion around the world, and particularly in Europe, is pressing governments to support renewable energy projects
- Concerns regarding reliability of existing oil and gas supply from the troubled regions of exporting countries
- China factor: Chinese government and businesses are now front runners in installation and use of solar electricity generation plants.

China has virtually no lobbies of coal and gas industries, which might suppress the advancement of renewable energy projects. In the US, there is such lobby, which has been successful in the past. However, this time these lobbies will be helpless. If China's solar energy projects achieve electricity cost much lower than that of coal and gas power stations, the US and Europe would have no choice but to follow the suite. That is what globalisation effect is: one part of the globe inevitably affects all others.

Solar energy generation is the fasted growing industry in China. In 2013 its added capacity is the biggest in the world, equal to 12.9 GWt. With improved efficiency, combined with Chinese low labour cost, and prudent government policy, this country is going to surprise the world with its energy progress, and other achievements, which are the inevitable consequence of increased power supply.

Any prognosis of the future is based on some assumption. Solar energy proliferation is no exception. The calculation below are based on the following assumptions:

- Investment in solar energy will remain approximately the same as it is now
- Solar panel with 46% efficiency will reach mass production in 2018. The cost of single panel will remain the same as in 2013, or lower
- Solar panels will reach 95% efficiency in 2020. At that time there will be a need to provide energy storage, which will take about 25% of energy generation. The actual efficiency therefore assumed to be about 70%. The cost of panel will be the same as in 2013 or lower, but with higher efficiency.

Table 7 shows a simplified calculation of the world solar energy supply, developed with an assumption that only the panels with 46% efficiency will be in production.

Table 8. Future of solar energy electricity generation.

Year	Investment bill. $	Commercial efficiency %	Added capacity GW per year	Added GW per period	Accum. Total
2013					138
2013-2018	112	15	38*	190	328
2018-2030	112	46	114	1368	1,696

* Source: Ren21-net

In average, each year capacity added is three times more than in 2013. In 2030 it will amount 1,696 GW.

If 95% efficiency materialises in 2020, and 70% is achieved after energy loss, as assumed above, the forecast is different, as shown in the table 7.

Table 9. Energy generation with maximum 70% efficiency of solar cells by 2030:

Year	Investment bill. $	Commercial efficiency %	Added GW per year	Added GW per period
2013				138
2013	112	15	38	38
2013-2018	112	15	38	190
2018-2020	112	46	114	228
2020-2030	112	70	175	1750
Total				2,344

In 2014, the world total electricity installed capacity in 2014 was 5,250 GWt.

Energy demand in 2030 will be only 36% higher then in 2014. This is due to the new trend - declining energy intensity, which is the amount of energy consumed per unit of GDP. Therefore, by 2030 the world will need 5,250 x 1.36 = 7,140 GW. The share of solar industry capacity in the total world demand will depend on the efficiency, achieved by the industry. The two scenarios, 46% and 70% capacity, is summarised in the table 10.

Table 10. Share of solar energy capacity in the total demand depending on efficiency achieved by the industry.

Efficiency %	World GWt	Solar GWt	% of world capacity
46	7,140	1696	23
70	7,140	2306	32

There are many pitfalls on the way of renewable energy progress. Among the major ones are the following:

- Declining policy support
- Electric grid-related constrains
- Opposition in some countries from electric utilities concerned about rising competition
- Continuing high global subsidies for fossil fuels

However, the writing is on the wall. There are some countries, which pioneered the progress of renewable energy sources and set fossil fuel reduction targets, shown in Table 11.

Table 11. Targets of renewables in selected countries

Göteborg, Sweden	100% of total energy fossil fuel-free by 2050
Madrid, Spain	20% reduction in fossil fuel use by 2020 (base 2004)
Seoul, South Korea	30% reduction in fossil & nuclear energy use by 2030 (base 1990)
Växjö, Sweden	100% of total energy fossil fuel-free by 2030
Vijayawada, India	10% reduction in fossil fuel use by 2018 (base 2008)

There are other cities, countries and municipalities around the globe, who set realistic targets of renewable energy use. This was unthinkable in the recent past, as it was prohibitively expensive. Now, it is already within the reach, and soon, with accelerated speed of technological advancement, may become even the best option available.

This is well worded in the summary of Augors report: "Solar photovoltaic is already today a low cost renewable energy technology. Most scenarios fundamentally underestimate the role of solar power in future energy systems."

Solar energy industry develops in combination with other sources of renewable energy, such as wind, hydro and nuclear. In order to forecast the future of energy, this issues have to be addressed to clarify the mechanism of future social and industrial changes, and interrelations among different factors.

How much power humanity can extract from solar energy without negatively affecting biological life on the planet Earth?

As any occurrence in the universe, it subjects to the phenomenon of large numbers. At the moment, there are some disagreements among scientists, but the unanimous consensus is that there is a long way to go before the impact will be noticed. However, the conversion of sun energy does interfere with the natural process of ecological cycles. As NASA Earth Observatory puts it, "When a flow of incoming solar energy is balanced by an equal flow of heat in space, Earth is in radiative equilibrium, and global temperature is relatively stable. Anything that increases or decreases the amount of incoming or outgoing energy disturbs Earth's relative equilibrium, global temperature must rise or fall in response."

Chapter 4. Wind Energy

Wind power is an obvious candidate for cheap energy generation. So, what's the problem? Why it was not used widely before fossil fuel burning engines were invented? Wouldn't it be simpler? After all, even in the distant past, when technology was primitive, wind was used to propel marine vessels by sails, and provide power for windmills in medieval times. Why not utilise its force for electricity generation? The energy is clean, abundant, free for all, and causes no pollution or any harmful impact on the environment. Only in the last two decades the wind technology began gathering steam, and in 2005 it reached the volume of industrial development. It turned out that its harvesting was, and still is, a combination of enormous technological, political, financial, and administrative challenges.

Here are just the most evident:

Wind is not always blowing. Everyone knows this simple fact, but for the wind turbine it means that it would not generate electricity in quiet periods. Therefore, other sources should be available to ensure uninterrupted supply of electricity at such times at these locations.

Wind may pick up at night, or at other times, when electricity consumption is low. Therefore, electricity generated at such times must be either directed to the grid, or stored somehow for future use. It was, and is, a serious challenge for the industry. The reason was not only technical sophistication: enormous capital was required for this task, which became available only when the industry matured and became competitive.

Beside energy storage, balancing supply and demand could be achieved by building transmission lines between geographical areas of wind facilities. The wind intensity is different at different times and at different locations. To smooth out electricity supply, electricity from the area of intensive wind could be transmitted to the one with low intensity wind.

In some locations, availability of a hydro station is the best solution. When wind generated electricity exceeds the local needs, a hydro station can reduce its output or temporarily shut down to store the rising water for future use. This way no additional expense is required to balance electricity supply.

Another way of energy storage is to build artificial water reservoir feeding a hydro power station. Whenever wind, or other renewable energy source generate excessive electricity, it can be used to pump water into this reservoir, and later use it for hydro electricity generation when wind or solar power is the lowest. Usually it incurs about 25% loss of generated electricity.

There are other ideas around, but all of them require large investments in R&D and implementation. But not only the availability of capital is the culprit. The cost of wind produced electricity was much higher than that generated by burning fossil fuel. Why bother?

In early eighties, a meteoric rise of China's economy had begun. Many third world countries followed the suit. Consumption of fossil fuel skyrocketed, and with it the price of oil and gas. As the price of oil went up, gigantic wind projects started: in a few years the progress of wind technology to prominence had begun, as shown in the Chart 3.

Chart 3. Wind Global Power Capacity.

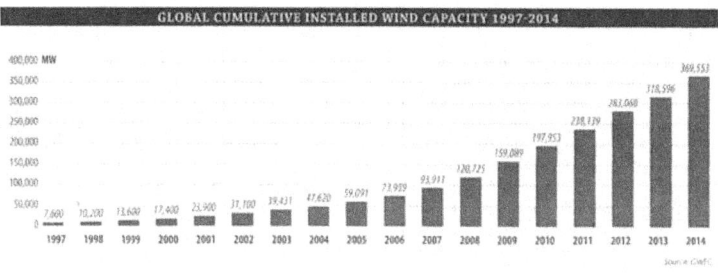

There are a few important factors, affecting development of wind technology.

First, increased efficiency of wind turbines. Its progress leads to reduced cost per watt of electricity. It also works in close relation with the economy of scale; the larger the production of wind infrastructure elements, the less expensive they become, thus the less is the cost of generated energy.

So far as levelized cost of wind generated electricity, its calculation is very tricky. Many factors influence it in various degrees. Price fluctuation of commodities, particularly steel and copper at the time of manufacture, price of energy for producing wind power infrastructure, intensity of wind at different locations, affecting turbine design and cost, are just to name a few. There are also natural constrains of geography, where wind turbines are installed. According to Wind Energy Foundation, "...wind turbines operate over a limited range of wind speeds. If the wind is too slow, they won't be able to turn, and if too fast, they shut down to avoid being damaged. Ideally, a wind turbine should be matched to the speed and frequency of the resource to maximize power production."

At a typical wind farm, most time the wind speed is between 3 to 10 m/sec. But the maximum energy is produced at the speed between 7 to 17 meters per second.

Nonetheless, the levelized cost of wind electricity is expected to decline till 2030 and beyond. There is a theoretical limit of this cost though, which may somehow affect proliferation of wind technology in the future.

Currently, the price of wind generated electricity in the US (in 2011-2012), according to Wind Energy Foundation "…averaged just 4 cents per kilowatt hour, which is 50% lower than in 2009".

The cost of wind fuel is zero, "so the price of electricity from a wind farm is predictable over the long term—which is not true for any fuelled power plant."

This factor should not be underestimated. Those countries which want to reduce dependence on oil and gas, and stay away from upheavals in the oil producing countries, may opt for wind power even if it is more expensive than the one produced by gas-oil-coal power stations.

As the price of electricity is known, a long term – 15 years or more – contract can be signed between suppliers and consumers. Therefore, the existing levelized method of cost calculation does not make sense, as fossil fuel prices are not predictable long term. This is also one of the reason for many countries to opt for wind power generation.

Dependence on fossil fuel in developed world was a cause of irritation, and often pain. Poor countries, rich with oil, dictated oil price with no relation to the economy of extraction, and often dictated their terms of international policy to the developed world. The fossil fuel itself, even if it was in abundance, is another cause of frustration. Its pollution and contamination of environment causes epidemic of illnesses, most of which were rare in the past. Without exaggeration, the very existence of humanity is now in danger. There are ways to reduce pollution to manageable level, but in the past the anti-pollution laws have not been properly enforced. Cleaning technology is very expensive; fully implemented, it would make electricity price skyrocket, thus negatively affecting economy, employment, and living standard. In a way, developed world chose the way of prosperity, sacrificing their physical health, and disregarding its harmful affect on future generations. Now, as public is aware of it, it is in favour of renewable energy. Particularly so at locales where the cost of renewable energy is comparable, or even lower, than the cost of fossil fuel generated electricity.

The policy toward wind technology differs from one country to another. Governments consider availability of fossil fuel on their territory, availability of wind – its consistency and periods of the most usable speed – and availability of alternative sources, which will provide the power when supply from wind generated electricity is low.

The leader in wind technology, by various estimates, is China. With meteoric growth of its manufacturing output and energy consumption since 1980, it became the largest importer of oil in the world. Its dependence on import reached a level dangerous to its economy and security. Thus, in 2010, of 455 tons of consumed oil China imported over 200 million tons. (Wikipedia, Petroleum Industry in China). The government undertakes frantic measures to insure safe import from abroad, but at the same time promotes supply of renewable energy, so abundant in this country. In the last few years China has been the leader of the world in new additions of wind energy. In 2013 it added 16.1 GW, totalling around 90 GW.

China has another incentive to use wind energy: air pollution from fossil fuel in China is the largest in the world. China's population is increasingly intolerant to the harmful environment. A new generation has grown up; it has new mentality and much less fear of the government than the previous generations. They demand better quality of life, and the quality of environment is the issue they address. The Chinese government now is as prudent as it has been in the last 35 years: it undertakes wise measures to ensure political stability, economic growth, and independence from all supply channels of the world. This is not to say that it is an exemplary good government. China could – and, my personal opinion, will - shudder the world in the future with its policy and might. But to be objective, we have to give it a credit and recognize its achievements.

Together with other countries of the region, which are also concerned about stability of oil supply, this part of the globe is the most advanced.

This development likely to influence the price of oil in the future. The less dependent Asian countries become from the world oil supply, the lower might (not necessarily will) be the price of oil. This, in turn, will provide less incentives for business to use renewable energy, as the fuel burning facilities may provide less expensive alternative. Again, all depends on governments policy, which may consider harmful affect of fossil fuels burning, and cost of cleaning the environment.

This is as far as installed capacity is concerned. However, the same installed capacity may produce different amount of energy: it depends on availability of wind, its speed, and some other factors. In terms of *energy produced*, the US is still the leader in the world in the field of wind technology.

The well-established trend of wind technology progress in China is expected to move on with increasing velocity. China has no fossil fuel lobby; it does not have an abundance of oil and gas reserves. The final decision in China therefore, whether influenced by policy or economy, is up to the Chinese government. The statistics shows that it moves in the direction of increased use of renewable energy. At present, the wind energy in China became the larges source of electricity after coal and hydro-electric power. As of 2014, China was an undisputed leader in the world for the total installed capacity, as shown in Table 12.

Table 12. Wind Energy Worldwide

Pos. 2013	Country/Region	Total MW 2014	Added 2014	Growth 2014 %
1	China	114,763	23,350	25.7
2	USA	65,879	4,854	7.8
3	Germany	40,468	5,808	16.8
4	Spain	22,987	27.5	16.8
5	India	22,465	2,315	11.5
6	UK	11,998	1,467	13.9
7	Canada	9,694	1,871	25.9
8	France	9,296	1,042	12.6
9	Italy	8,663	107.5	1.3
10	Brazil	6,182	2,783	81.9
11	Sweden	5,425	1,050	21.4
12	Denmark	4,850	78	1.6
	Rest of the world	47,300	51,753	16
	Total	370,000	51,753	16.2

With many large projects in the pipeline, China will be able to reduce the cost of wind power hardware due to its mass production. This, in turn, will reduce the cost of electricity generation, whereby making it competitive with the cheapest fuel burning power stations.

There is enough data to predict the future of wind power technology. The most realistic projection in our opinion was made by GWEC, reflected in its 2015 report. It offers three scenarios: New Policy Scenario, Moderate scenario, and Advanced Scenario. Although Advanced Scenario has the best chance to be the most accurate, as preceding exhibits and government targets suggests, I opt to select the Moderate Scenario, just not to be overly optimistic. It gives the total electricity production in the world in TWh (Table 13).

Table 13. Wind Power Electricity Production forecast

Year	Global cumulative capacity GW	Production TWh	% of World Electricity
2013	318	620	2.9
2015	413	1,013	4.9
2020	712	1,747	7.2
2025	1,073	2,631	
2030	1,480	3,889	12.9
2035	1,804	4,740	
2040	2,089	5,491	15.2
2045	2,374	6,238	
2050	2,672	7,023	17.0

The most essential data in this table is production TWh. This is the amount of electricity delivered by whatever capacity is installed. As the table suggests, the world electricity demand by the year 2030 will be much greater than BP report – mentioned before - suggests.

According to this table, wind electricity production by the year 2030 will increase from the base of 2013 in 6.3 times. However, its percentage of penetration will increase in about 4.4 times. Another words, the world demand will grow much faster than the growth of wind electricity generation. It has not been the case up until

2015. Statistics shows much faster wind technology growth. So far its capacity doubles in each 3 years.

Dynamics of renewable energy growth, particularly wind and solar generated electricity, may make an impression that humanity has found a panacea for most of its energy problems. The energy is abundant, free, and harmless. What could be better?

The reality is not quite that rosy. Scientists and engineers point out that the space for wind infrastructure is not endless. Wind turbines should not be positioned to close to one another as the wind, in its most efficient speed range, looses most of its energy after exiting the blades. Therefore, its diminishing strength would produce much less electricity when hitting the blades of the subsequent rows of turbines, thereby reducing efficiency and increasing the cost of generated electricity.

There is another surprising, and quite unexpected consequence of wind energy production: a potential harmful affect of this industry on global environment. As everything in reality, if a number of occurrence gets large enough, at certain point it produces effect much larger than the preceding occurrences suggest. In mathematics it is a well-studied phenomena: large numbers lead to unpredictable consequences. Wind technology, as any other developments, is not an exception.

To demonstrate this point, let us consider a simple example. A small warehouse receive 10 pieces of a part from one supplier, and sells it to two different manufacturers. In this case only one stock keeper can easily handle all paper work, and associated administration. If the number of this part grows to 100 pieces per day, its registration, tracking of its movement, recording its location in the stock room, and other tasks needs significant work force. If, however, the number increases to 1000 pieces per day, a complex combination

41

of administration and computer technology, and automation is required to handle the task. Moreover, new problems appear, such as calculating probability of ordering quantity from different manufacturers, automatic reordering system, and many others. And if we add to that a few more supplies and manufacturers, the task of handling only one part grows to gigantic undertaking. And this is only for one part!

We reached the stage when humanity, in its attempt to solve its problems, has to deal with global consequences. Some of them we already know, but many are for future discoveries.

Thus, we still don't know how proliferation of wind (and solar) technology will affect environment. Considering this, one point must be clearly understood: the nature never gives a free lunch.

Interesting research was conducted at the Max-Plank-Institute of biochemistry in Germany. According to it, biological environment on Earth is an integrated process, in which sun, wind and waves take part in ecological rejuvenation. Energy availability from wind and waves is limited: too much extraction of it therefore might negatively affect its regeneration, thereby breaking natural cycle of biological life on the Earth. Using sophisticated mathematical models scientists of this institute arrived at the conclusion that the natural ability of the Earth's system to generate energy from wind is 1,000 Terawatt. As the report puts it, "Hence a renewable source of energy based on wind and waves is continually replenished by energy input from the sun, but ultimately finite." And further to the point: "…extracting the maximum power from the Earth's wind would have the same impact on climate change as a doubling in atmospheric carbon dioxide."

Is 1,000 Terawatt is too much or too little?

The IEA estimate for 2012 is, that humanity consumption of energy was close to 20 Terawatts. This encompasses all energy use: fossil fuel burning for electricity production, in combustion engines, solar, wind, nuclear and all other kinds of energy. There is a long way to go to 1,000 Terawatts available for harvesting. Our calculations in the last chapter of this work suggests that humanity would never ever reach this level of energy consumption.

Interesting conclusion was made at Stanford Report, published on September 10, 2012. Although the wind potential is great, it is not endless. "At some point, however, the return on building new turbines would plateau, reaching a level in which no additional energy could be extracted with installation of more turbines." Here the phenomena of large numbers comes into effect: "Each turbine reduces the amount of energy available for others. The reduction, however, becomes significant only when large numbers of turbines are installed, many more than would ever be needed."

The paper gives the following estimate:

- The saturated potential is more than 250 terawatts. Less than Max-Plank-Institute number, but still far beyond contemporary needs of humanity
- 4 million turbines, each operating at a height of 100 meters producing 5 MW could supply as much as 7.5 terawatts – close to half of all-purpose world energy demand
- 2 million turbines would be installed over water, and 2 million on the land, taking about 1 percent of the Earth's land surface

How will wind and solar technology impact the life of humanity in the next 15 years? To what extent? And what will happen in the more distant future? These issue are considered in the next chapters.

Chapter 5. Wind and Solar Technology in the Near Future

For calculations supporting arguments in this chapter please refer Appendix 1. They clarify the logic employed to predict the outcome of already established trends.

Suppose the world community unanimously decided to substitute the fossil fuel generated electricity with the wind and solar energy. As calculation in Appendix 1 shows, in this case in 2030 the solar and wind generated electricity output should reach approximately 19,391 TWh. If the ratio between the wind and solar energy would remain in 2030 the same as it is in 2014, then the wind generated electricity should be 13,497 TWh (see Table A1-5), and the solar generated electricity should be 5,471 TWh. To achieve this, the world should invest total $9,906 billions (almost 10 trillion dollars) in wind, and $5,382 billions (more that 5 trillion dollars) in solar energy, assuming that a few years from now the efficiency of solar panels will reach 46%. Thus, total investment in these technologies must be approximately $15,377 billions in 17 years, or $905 billions each year during this period – an astronomical, unrealistic amount, if compared with the contemporary investments.

It is, however, reasonable to assume that investment in these technologies will remain close to what has been reported in the last few years, as both industries are approaching to maturity. With the investment of $80 billion per year in wind, and $112 billion in solar technology, it would take 124 years for wind, and 49 years for solar technology to reach capability to produce the target amount of energy.

Resolving energy issue, however, requires much more than just increasing energy supply for a theoretically calculated level. To demonstrate that, let's assume, just for an intellectual exercise, that humanity would substitute fossil fuel with the wind and solar technology for electricity generation by 2030. Would it diminish the total fossil fuel consumption in comparison with the 2015 level? Would it push the oil price down? The answer is a big NO!

In 2013, the global production of oil reached 86.8 million barrels a day. Just 5 percent of it was used for electricity production. The BP report forecasts 36 percent increase of the world GDP in 2030. If oil consumption grows in step with GDP, then in 2030 the oil production should be 36 percent more, which is 118.05 million barrels a day. If 5 percent of oil, currently used for electricity production, is excluded from this number – since all fossil fuels will be replaced by renewables – then the total world consumption must be 113 million barrels per day.

So, in spite of impressive advance of solar and wind technology, the world's dependence on oil will increase from 94.0 million barrels per day (as in 2015) to 112.96 million barrels per day in 2030.

Energy is the substance which it is never enough, no matter how much and how cheap it is. Energy is the essence of everything produced. Eventually, the cost of any product is the result of used energy. If energy gets less expensive, people buy more material things, thereby driving the price of all products up. People want bigger houses, bigger cars, more cars, more anything that is out there at the markets. This buying frenzy results in increasing demand for energy. When supply and demand get out of balance, the price of energy goes up.

The major consumer of oil is transportation in all its variety. Its share in oil consumption grows faster than consumption in other industries. In 2013, distribution of oil consumption worldwide was as shown in Table 14.

Table 14. Share of transportation in global oil consumption

Type of usage	% in total
Road transportation	43
Industry	16
Residential/commercial/agriculture	11
Petrochemicals	10
Electricity generation	7
Aviation	6
Marine bunkers	5
Waterways/rail	3

The share of transportation in the total oil use has been increasing since 1973. Obsession with cars is not just the psychological phenomena. With the contemporary trend of expanding suburban life in the developed world, a car is a necessity. So far there is no feasible alternative to the fossil fuel burning engine. Until road transportation energy alternatives are found, oil supply will remain the major economic problem for the whole world. The issue is therefore, the future of oil supply. What oil price could be expected? Would world supply be disrupted for some political or economical reason? Would price of oil jump to the new height, thus bringing the world economy to a severe crises?

Before addressing these questions, the associated issue has to be explained: what caused the sudden drop of oil price at the end of 2014? How long this low price will stay? What implications are for the world economy and politics if the price of oil remains for long at the present level?

Chapter 6. Shale oil production and its short and long term impact on oil supply

Shale oil belongs to the transient category. Its influence on the oil price is temporary. Its economically recoverable reserves are limited. Under any circumstances, considering growing demand for fuel till 2030, its share in the total liquid fuel production will be diminishing, thereby its production volume will affect the oil price in a lesser degree. Its technically recoverable deposits are much smaller than that of conventional oil, and "...corresponds to around 10% of all global technically recoverable resources of oil (conventional and unconventional) as estimated by the U.S. Energy Information Administration (2013)."

Oil is a unique product. Beside being the obvious power for transportation, it is used in agriculture for production of fertilizers, in manufacturing for production of plastics, machinery parts, construction elements, fabrics for textile industry, and in numerous other applications. For transportation though, as it stands now, it is the primary source of energy: this sector consumes 55 percent of extracted oil world wide, although this number varies from country to country. Thus, in the US, the transportation sector consumes 68 percent of its used oil.

The importance of transportation is impossible to underestimate: without it economic activity would collapse. That is why oil availability and production is of geopolitical impotence.

The oil price jump close to $140 per barrel in 2008 was regarded by many as an exaggerated reaction to unbalanced supply and demand. Pessimistic forecasts were abound. However, there were some who took it as a trend into the future. But at the end of 2014, the oil price dropped below $50 per barrel. This stirred a heated debate about the cause, affect, and future of oil supply and demand. It comes as no surprise that some predicted long years of a new era: cheap oil, prosperity in developed world, and turmoil for most oil producing countries as a logical outcome of reduced revenue.

For better understanding of the future of oil it is necessary to briefly overview the two concepts: Peak Oil Production theory, and the notion of diminishing, and progressively more energy consuming extraction of energy resources.

The Peak Oil Production theory, first proposed in the early 20th century, gathered recognition in the 1950s. It claims that the world oil production would reach its peak at some point in time, stay briefly at the peak plateau, and then will begin its steady and steep decline. The theory explicitly excludes all non-conventional oils: shale oil, sand oil, biofuels, and other liquid products.

There are two primary considerations that support this theory. As statistics demonstrates, the largest oil discoveries have already been made. Most experts agree on that, as demonstrated in the Business Week's article *Peak Oil: Information and Strategies*: "It is now widely acknowledged by the world's leading petroleum geologists that more than 95 percent of all recoverable [conventional] oil has now been found."

These deposits are quickly depleting, and the remaining oil is progressively more difficult to extract. In the same article the author says: "Worldwide discovery of oil peaked in 1964 and has followed a steady decline since." By various estimates it was in the range of 55-60 billion barrels. As 95 percent of all known reserves are in production, few major discoveries remain to be made.

Exploration of new reserves is a labour intensive task. For any new discovery it takes more time and effort to extract oil from it than it had taken for earlier easy finds. No matter how many new finds are out there, their production does not offset the diminishing output of the old reserves.

Peak Oil Production theory claims that these two trends accelerate. At some point the new discoveries will offset diminishing output of old reserves, and the total production will level out. How long would it last is anybody's guess, but inevitably this plateau will be followed by diminishing production regardless of effort put into new exploration.

King Hubert, the author of this theory, forecasted this peak at 12.5 billion barrels in the year 2000. This is approximately 34,250 million barrels per day. He was wrong at that. The real production far exceeded this number, however flattened out in the last 10 years.

Opponents of Peak Oil Production theory used statistics of the early 2000s to claim that the oil production peak would never happen. And yet, as production data accumulates, proofs supporting this theory is hard to dismiss.

The most convincing indicator of diminishing production of any reserve is the amount of energy produced for one unit of energy extracted. It is called EROEI – Energy Returned On Energy Invested. The greater the number, the more energy efficient is oil production. Statistics shown in Table 15 demonstrated a steady acceleration of its decline.

Table 15. Barrels of oil produced on one barrel used.

Year	EROEI
1920+	100:1
1950+	20:1
2010+	9:1
New reserves-conventional oil	5:1
Non-conventional oil (shale, sand, other)	4:1

The table confirms the obvious: the cost of energy – the key component of energy economy – is on the rise. Progressively more energy is required to extract a unit of production (or less energy produced for a unit of energy spent).

Here is a quote from *The Energy Cost of Production. Global Nation*: "Back in the 1920s, oil was paying off at 100-to-1. It took one barrel of oil to extract, process, refine, ship and deliver 100 barrels of oil. That's a phenomenal rate of return. If you work out of the percentage, that's a 10,000 percent rate of return."

The relations between EROEI to dollar cost of extracted unit is not linear. Thus, the energy cost of conventional oil production now is at EROEI = 9, and its dollar cost, according to Paris based IEA, is $10-$25. With EROEI=4 for shale oil formations, production cost of a barrel is $50-$100, which is 4-5 times higher.

At the time of this writing the only disagreement among the theory proponents is about the timing of the Peak Oil Production. Some geologists ascertain that we have already reached it. Others, more optimistic, forecast it for 2020. Thereafter, the conventional oil production will enter the final phase of steady decline. To sum up, the obvious evidence is:

- Existing oil reserves deplete faster than the new reserves are found
- Discovery of new reserves is more labour intensive, as the largest and easiest reservoirs of oil have already been found
- The new discoveries do not offset declining output of the existing wells
- The oil from the old reserves takes more energy to extract. Statistics demonstrate that the effectiveness of production is on a steady decline.
- The same is true for the new found reserves.

Pessimistic view would have been remarkably accurate if not for the US shale oil production, thanks to which the total US crude oil production reached 9.2 million barrels per day in 2015.

The consensus among experts is that the US shale oil production was the primary cause of the sharp drop in oil prices in 2014. To better understand it and its connection with Peak Oil Production, a broad picture of the world supply and demand dynamics must be considered.

The Table 16 shows total world liquids and oil production from different sources, and conventional oil production.

Table 16. World Oil Production Statistics

Year	Daily Mb/Day – total liquids *	Daily Mb/day total oils**
2004	80.938	70,706
2005	81.963	72,176
2006	82.417	71,945
2007	82.220	71,611
2008	82.847	72,581
2009	81.149	71,317
2010	83.190	73,216
2011	83.980	73,485
2012	86.150	75,063
2013	86.579	75,239
2014	88.673	74.28

* BP statistical review of world energy June 2015. Includes all liquids.
** EIA

Whatever interpretation of these numbers might be, it is evident that the difference between the total oil production and total liquid production is increasing. This difference is attributed to the output of alternative liquids, including shale oil. If shale oil is excluded from total oil production, we can clearly identify a plateau of oil production around 70 million barrels per day. Most of shale oil is currently extracted in the US.

As *Energy Trend Insider* stated, "Just to put the current US oil boom into further perspective, over the past five years global oil production has increased by 3.85 million barrels per day. During that same time span, US production increased by 3.22 million bpd — 83.6 percent of the total global increase. Had the US shale oil boom never happened and US production continued to decline as it had for nearly 40 years prior to 2008, the global price of oil might easily be at \$150 to \$200 a barrel by now. Without those additional barrels on the market from (primarily) North Dakota and Texas, the price of crude would have risen until supply and demand were in balance."

In the U.S., the plateau of conventional oil production is evident. It remains at the level of 2005-2008: in all likelihood it will be followed by ever increasing decline of production. As IEA 2014 report stated, "Without the 3.5 Mb/d added from shale formations the US crude oil production would be around 5 Mb/d around the level of 2008 average annual production."

As the oil price dropped, a chores of optimists exploded with jubilant prediction of almost unlimited affordable energy supply, and low oil price. A good example of it is the article *2012 Oil Shale & Tar Sands Programmatic EIS*, referring to the Rand Corporation report(19): "Present U.S. demand for petroleum products is about 20 million barrels per day. If oil shale could be used to meet a quarter of that demand, the estimated 800 billion barrels of recoverable oil from the Green River Formation would last for more than 400 years."

If. That's the question. Implications, of course, are enormous: end of developed world's dependence on Middle East and Russia oil supply, restructure of global policy, and long stretch of prosperity. Is that so?

There are two broad categories of shale oil deposits: technically recoverable resources and economically recoverable resources. Technically recoverable resource is defined as recoverable with the known technology, regardless of economics.

Economically recoverable resource can be extracted with profit under existing economic conditions. These deposits are much smaller than technically recoverable ones. Many profound technical issues, as well as geological reality, stand on the way of converting technically recoverable resource to economically recoverable resource.

Shale oil is not a liquid substance. Although it is of organic origin, as the conventional oil, but heat and pressure at the time of its formation was not high enough, and the substance became a solid rock. As it can not be pumped as conventional oil, the rock must be either liquefied or converted to gas for extraction.

Technology of shale oil extraction is a miracle of human intellect. A vertical well up to 3 kilometers deep (or more) must be drilled. It must be insulated from underground water to prevent contamination. Then, depending on testing results, a horizontal tunnel, usually from 1 to 3 km. long, must be drilled, but sometimes the tunnel stretches as far as 6 kilometers. Only then a water based solution is injected under high pressure to extract oil.

According to IEA 2013, the global technically recoverable shale oil is 345 Gb (Giga barrels). By comparison, world conventional oil reserves as of 2007 are 1,238 Gb.

Table 17 shows the top 10 countries with technically recoverable shale oil resource estimates.

Table 17. Top 10 countries with technically recoverable shale oil reserves

Country	Unproven shale oil technically recoverable resources (Gb)
Russia	75
U.S.	58
China	32
Argentina	27
Libia	26
Australia	18
Venezuela	13
Mexico	13
Pakistan	9
Canada	9

So, it seems that it is just the matter of technology advancement to the point when technically recoverable resource will be upgraded to economically recoverable resource. Is it possible? Do these numbers mean that we have arrived at the era of abundant oil, and political stability for developed world? Is technology of shale oil extraction will be improving indefinitely?

Not that simple: there are numerous factors affecting the price and volume of oil shale production. These issues were discussed in depth by top notch experts in shale oil industry, Chris Martenson and David Hughes, published in Peak Prosperity (34).

According to them, the richest deposits of shale oil in the U.S. are in Bakken play. In it, wells registered an average of 45% annual field production decline. The biggest decline happens in the first year: it is about 70%, however it slows in following years. According to experts' calculations, it is necessary to drill 1500 wells per year just to keep the production flat. As the average cost is $10 million per well, $15 billion must be spent to maintain the current volume of extraction. This is for the richest reserve, which contains only half of the sweet spot. As the best spots are the first to explore, less productive spots are down the road. When production moves to lower quality deposits, about 3000 wells in a year must be drilled just to keep the production flat. To increase production, more wells are needed.

The shale oil availability and its future pricing is of vital importance for the whole world. As shale boom in the U.S. is so heavy a part of the equation, the question narrows down to: how long the shale boom will last? Is it possible to forecast the range of oil price fluctuations till 2030? What will happen with energy resources in the more distant future?

With the advent of shale oil production the mechanism of conventional oil pricing has changed. Its rise is limited by the average cost of shale oil production. As soon the oil price grows higher then the cost of shale oil production, the size of economically recoverable reserves will expand, and production of shale oil will increase. Therefore, at least for the near future, the cost of shale extraction will define the price of oil on international markets.

According to Scotiabank Equity Research, the weighted average cost of North American shale oil is about $60 per barrel. It is therefore reasonable to assume that the shale oil price will not rise significantly above $60 - $70 per barrel as long as the shale "revolution" will march on, and no major political turmoil and disruption occurs in the Middle East.

There is a serious problem with the validity of the weighted average cost: it does not reflect the true cost of shale oil extraction. Sooner or later, the damage to the environment, repairs of ruined transportation infrastructure, and use of other resources, like water, will be accounted for, and this will drive the cost of shale oil production to new heights. The question therefore is, what is the true cost of shale oil extraction? Is it possible to calculate it with a reasonable approximation?

A few primary factors must be taken into account. There are thousands of heavy trucks moving around daily with shale oil and waste. Their stress on roads, bridges and other elements of transportation infrastructure takes its toll, but oil companies do not pay for their repair and maintenance. The environment cleaning expenses are not included in the price of oil as well. Information on all damages and consequences of shale oil extraction is still sporadic and inaccurate, but some reliable data emerge. Thus, in Texas, the Department of Transportation estimated that 4 billion dollars of road damage is done by oil and gas trucks *each year*.

In 2013, one million barrels per day was produced in the region. Therefore, in the whole year 365 million barrels was produced. This means that transportation infrastructure damage in a single year was $4,000/365 = $10.96 per barrel. According to official statistics Eagle Ford Formation shale oil cost $40-$60 per barrel. If the expense of road infrastructure damage is included, the cost will increase to $50-$70 per barrel. If cleaning environment expenses are also included in the cost of oil, it would be higher, but at present there is no sufficient data for exact calculations. However, experts say that the environmental impact of this technology is severe; water pollution, poisonous gas emission, waste, etc.

There are also talks about the loss of water in the process of shale extraction. For each barrel of produced oil, 1-4 barrels of water is required. This water is lost forever: it is impossible to recover it from such depth. Is it a lot to worry about?

As exact aggregate data does not exist, I take a conservative estimate of 2 barrels of water per one barrel of oil. Contemporary production of shale oil in the U.S. is approximately 4 million barrels per day. For this volume, 8 million barrels of water per day must be used. For a year, 8 x 365 = 2,920 million barrels (2.9 billion), or 348,182 million liters, will be used. This is 0.348 cubic kilometers. In the next 10 years it will be about 3.5 cubic kilometers. Is it a lot?

For comparison, lake Tahoe contains 150.7 cubic kilometers of water. In my opinion, water consumed by shale oil extraction does not amount to ecological disaster. However, the final say is for environmentalists.

The price of water is difficult to calculate, particularly so if it is lost forever from the surface of Earth. Now it is, in most locations, free for oil companies. If they are charged as much as population, the price of shale oil will be much higher.

There is a rising opposition of experts against the shale oil extraction the way it is. It is reasonable to expect increased taxation on shale oil and gas extraction to offset damages. Therefore the weighted average cost of shale oil production will increase to at least $70-$80 per barrel, if not more.

If the US government policy toward shale oil producing companies remain the same and no charges for environmental and infrastructure damages are laid, the price of oil is unlikely to rise above $70 per barrel. But the damage is quite obvious, and taxpayers are unlikely remain the willing partner to foot the bill.

The experts claim that the existing well productivity has already peaked. New wells are of poor quality and therefore less productive. The expert's conclusion is that the total shale output will peak before 2020. After that, two factors will influence the price of oil: increasing demand and decreasing production.

In 2007, the total world oil production from all sources was 86 million barrels per day. But, according to the BP forecast, the global number of cars on roads will increase form 1 billion as of now to 2.4 billions in 2030 – 2035. This will raise the demand for fuel. However, demand of agriculture and industry for petroleum products will also increase due to fast increasing human population. Consumption of oil is expected to rise to 120 mln. barrels a day. As the oil output flattens in early 2020, the oil price will raise above the weighted average cost of shale oil, and continue to climb in line with decreasing shale and conventional oil production.

So far, we considered only U.S. shale oil production. But there are significant shale oil deposits around the globe. If explored, they may influence the price of oil as well. But, according to experts, it is unlikely to happen.

The shale oil deposits in Europe are not large, but it has rich deposits of shale gas. Their exploration in the near future though is not likely. Experts almost unanimously agree that the US will remain the only country which extracts oil from shale formations in significant quantity. According to Linnea Lung, there are reasons "why the shale revolution in North America will not easily be repeated in Europe. Firstly, the U.S. shale revolution did not come out of nowhere – decades of geological exploration preceded the boom of the first decade of 2000's. Between 2000 and 2010 a total of 17,268 exploratory gas wells were drilled in the US, as compared to about 50 wells drilled in the EU. There are many political and environmental issues, as well as public opposition, which often impossible to overcome on the way of commercial shale oil and gas production.".

In summary, the shale oil 'revolution' will not last long. By 2020, its share in total world production will drop. Consequently, the cost of its recovery, even in the best case scenario, will no longer be a factor influencing the international oil price. Unless there is a drastic breakthrough in other technologies, the price of oil will continue its climb up to new heights.

Chapter 7. Fuel Cell Technology

Problems, associated with fossil fuel burning are becoming critical for humanity with each passing year. Its poisonous affect on environment and health of biological life on the planted became evident, and needs to be addressed as the task of first priority. No less important is the fact that fossil fuel deposits are final and depleting at alarming rate. Its geological distribution is also a problem for many countries: any disturbance in the places of major deposits, or political decisions of oil producing countries may lead to significant disruption of world economy.

Particularly troublesome is the situation in transportation. Combustion engine, as it stands now, is the primary technology. Governments and businesses in many countries try their best to find administrative and technical solutions geared toward reducing fossil fuel consumption, such as:

- develop efficient public transportation
- provide incentives to use electric cars
- Use lighter material for building cars, thereby reducing power needed to propel a vehicle
- Design more efficient engines
- Improve design of electric cars and hybrids

And many others. But technical advancements, however great they might be, do not change the law of physics: any combustion process, used for generation of energy, including generation of electricity for electric cars, has maximum efficiency of about 42 percent.

As of 2015, the technological reality is that only fuel cell technology can break this theoretical limit and provide up to 90 percent efficiency when using fossil fuel for energy generation. In theory, solar energy could achieve similar results. However, as we discussed in the previous chapters, its share in the total energy demand is not going to be significant enough to affect oil price, or provide energy for mass production of electric cars in the foreseeable future.

Since yearly 1990s discussions about wonders of fuel cell technology has never stopped. R&D expenses in this field are enormous, and continue to grow by leaps and bounds. In practical terms, considering infrastructure and other losses, its efficiency now is around 70 percent. It is an enormous breakthrough of modern science and technology.

Fuel cells generate electricity by chemical reaction instead of combustion. Some fuel cells use hydrogen for this process, another use fossil fuel. Those using hydrogen emit pure water, thereby delivering clean energy.

All is good, but theoretical wonders of fuel cell technology is hard to bring about. Although the industry matures fairly quickly, the primary directions of its variations in terms of cost competitiveness is still uncertain.

To peek into the fuel cell technology future, it is necessary to make a quick overview of its technological varieties and their likely development.

For small vehicles, such as cars, scooters and motorcycles, scientists and engineers work on perfection of Proton Exchange Membrane Fuel Cell (PEMFC) engines. Its theoretical efficiency is about 83%, and some models promise even better, but so far in practice it is below 60 percent. The latest models though achieved 70%

efficiency, and in all likelihood, as automotive experts predict, it is going be the industry standard in the near future.

In the core of PEMFC is a chemical reaction between hydrogen and oxygen, which produces electric current and heat. In stationary applications this heat can be utilized to heat up water and houses. The emission is harmless as it is pure water. Because of the light weight, this type of fuel cell engine is a good candidate for transportation applications.

So far so good. But production and storage of hydrogen and cost of materials make this type of energy generation is more expensive than combustion engines. Particularly costly is a platinum catalyst. There are some promising attempts to substitute platinum with cheaper materials, but no practical solution has been found yet.

And last, but not the least, is the issue of producing hydrogen for fuel cells: at the time of writing it is expensive, and the process is associated with harmful pollution, perhaps even greater than that produced by combustion.

Even if the cost of materials drops and emission in hydrogen production reduced, the huge issue of coordination between governments and big business still remains. After all, as it stands now, about 1.2 billion cars worldwide are on the road, and uncountable motorcycles, scooters, millions of trucks, busses and other vehicles. Experts estimate that the number of vehicles will double by 2030, exceeding 2 billion units. Without coordinating policy required for replacement of humongous fleet of combustion engines, it would take many decades to make fuel cell engine a practical solution.

The evidence though is that in the last few years the technical, political and administrative plans began to emerge, and now the industry is advancing to mass production. According to industry spokesmen, small personal vehicles equipped with fuel cell generators will soon populate the roads of Japan, Germany, and other countries. It is expected that Asia scooters, so numerous in use there, will be powered by hydrogen fuel cell motors. This would reduce enormous poisonous pollution, produced by these vehicles, to zero.

Fuel cell engines proved to be a viable solution for large vehicles, such as busses and trucks. In this field, the larger the vehicle, the more efficient is the fuel cell application, and the more practical it become. In general, automotive industry experts and business people are rather optimistic, and have plans, funds and government support for large scale production. Is their optimism realistic? Facts demonstrate that it is.

First, there is an obvious trend of rapid reduction of energy cost, generated by a unit. Table 18 shows the progress of the cost dynamics from 2002, assuming that manufacturing volume is 500,000 units.

Table 18. Fuel Cell Cost Dynamics

Year	kW cost $
2002	275
2006	108
2007	94
2008	73
2009	61
2010	51
2011	49
2012	47
2017	30 (target)

The trend is similar to that of wind and solar energy. The most significant changes happened in the last few years. R&D data provides evidence that soon fuel cell technology will be competitive, and eventually less expensive than combustion engines.

In the recent past some economists argued that the cost of infrastructure for fuel cell vehicles will be prohibitively high. As recent data demonstrates, it is not nearly as much large undertaking as it seemed. Here is the quote from FCT_REVIEW_2015: "The cost of hydrogen infrastructure is modest by standards of energy and infrastructure spending, and no more than it is required for charging battery-electric vehicles. The Danes have calculated the public investment required to enable the production of FCEV [Fuel Cell Electric Vehicle] and the creation of the network between 2015 and 2025 (the point at which no further support is needed) is €345 million ($468 million) or as they put it, 'the cost of one bottle of wine for every Dane per year' over the period."

At the other end of the fuel cell technology spectrum is solid oxide fuel cells (SOFC). Without going into technical details, suffice it to mention that this technology operates at high temperature, usually in the range 500-1000 Celsius, and does not require hydrogen for fuel. Methane, propane, even biofuels can be used. The system does not need an expensive platinum catalyst, therefore is comparatively inexpensive in manufacture and operations. However, there are many other technical obstacles on the way to its mass production and use. If successfully resolved, they will open the way to competitive and cleaner electricity production, which in turn will prompt proliferation of electrical cars and support other applications, particularly those where electricity and heat are required.

There are other fuel cell varieties in between. Time will tell which one will be the leader in energy production. If and when a practical solution is found, fuel cell technology will solve numerous environmental problems, reduce consumption of fossil fuels, and revolutionize the existing system of electricity generation and distribution.

The most likely leader would be the SOFC fuel cell variety. There are a few reasons for this:

- No need to produce hydrogen as a fuel. It can operate on natural gas, propane, diesel, and pure and impure hydrogen
- Emissions can be reduced by more than 40 percent, depending on the fuel used
- Can integrate directly into existing fuel and electricity infrastructure
- Can be a local utility, thus eliminating needs for long-distance transmission lines from big power station. This will further reduce cost of electricity.

The biggest challenge of renewable source of energy technologies is energy storage. SOFC, in theory, provides solution for this. When electricity from the fuel cell generator is not required, it will be used to produce hydrogen from the surplus energy. As Mr. Andreas Benedict Richter, Manager at Business Development department at Topsoe Fuel Cell company explained, "Hydrogen can be stored under pressure and when needed re-converted to electricity using SOFC technology. The hydrogen is produced by reversing the function of the fuel cell in a so called electrolysis process. Instead of generating electricity from fuel with the by-products water and heat, the unit can be fed electricity, heat and steam to produce the hydrogen. This electrolysis is still in mere research phase and expected to move into commercialization soon after the break through of fuel cells"

What fuel cells gurus predict? If fuel cell technology delivers what it promises, we can expect huge energy savings, cheaper energy price and, as a consequence, a prolonged period of prosperity around the globe. Large scale implementation of SOFC fuel cells will "...extend the life of existing fuel reserves by at least 50 years. World wide savings will amount to 250,000 billion barrels."

It could have been true, if not for one factor, which has no numerical representation: human greed for more of everything. The more cheap energy a society produces, the more demand for its consumption develops. The most evident example is the life in America. Whenever opportunity exists, people buy bigger vehicles, build bigger houses, buy more things, travel and consume more. As production of consumer goods per unit gets cheaper, more things per consumer are bought. Consumption matches its steps with dynamics of energy cost, and often outpaces it. If policy toward energy consumption won't change in a profound way, humanity will never exit the vicious circle of incessant consumption and quickly diminishing energy resources.

Chapter 8. If Fuel Cell Technology is a Success

The question therefore is: when fuel cell technology will mature to be commercially competitive to the contemporary combustion technology? After all, oil reserves are depleting, whereas its consumption is on a steep rise. BP forecasts that in 2030 world daily oil production should reach 120 million barrels per day to satisfy the demand. A similar forecast is mentioned in Business Canada of July 27, 2015: "...a vehicle population of 2 billion would require the world to produce at least 120 million barrels per day, up from 87 million today." This is more than 30 million barrels a day than it is now. How fuel cell technology would affect this ever increasing balance deficit?

To better understand what 70 percent efficiency fuel cell technology means, consider the following example.

Suppose, we have 100 liters of gasoline at our disposal. A combustion engine of a car, with its efficiency of 40 percent, utilizes only 40 liters to propel the car. Remaining 60 liters are just waste.

If we use the same 100 liters in the fuel cell engine (or electric engine, whose electricity was produced by fuel cell generator) with 70% efficiency, then 70 liters will be used for driving the car, and 30 liters will be waste. Overall savings on the global scale will profoundly change the landscape of oil consumption. The following illustrates this point.

Petroleum products are used as transportation fuels, and also for heating and electricity generation, to produce asphalt and road oil, feedstock, to make chemicals, plastics, and synthetic materials found in nearly everything we use today. In 2013 the country used 6.89 billion barrels of petroleum. Their relative share of total U.S. petroleum consumption in 2013 was as in Table 19:

Table 19. Relative share of total U.S. petroleum consumption in 2013

Fuel type	Percent in total consumption
Gasoline	46
Heating Oil/Diesel Fuel	20
Jet Fuel (Kerosene)	8
Propane/Propylene	7
NGL & LRG	6
Still Gas	4
Petrochemical Feedstocks	2
Petroleum Coke	2
Residual/Heavy Fuel Oil	2
Asphalt and Road Oil	2
Lubricants	1
Miscellaneous Products/Special Naphthas	0.4
Other Liquids	1
Aviation Gasoline 0.1	0.1
Waxes	0.04
Kerosene	0.02

Gasoline and heating oil/diesel fuel used 66 percent of total oil consumed in 2013, which is 6.89:100x66= 4.55 billion barrels. With the contemporary 40 percent of combustion engine efficiency the productive liquid use is 1.82 billion barrels, and waste (60%) is 2.73 billion barrels.

With 70 percent efficiency of fuel cell technology the productive liquid use from the same total is 3,19 billion barrels, and waste is 1.37 billion barrels. Thus, the amount of gasoline used in contemporary technology in a year will be enough for about 1.75 years with fuel cell technology.

Globally, transportation accounts for 62.3 percent of petroleum consumption. By 2030, when the total petroleum consumption is expected to be 120 million barrels a day, combustion based transportation will use approximately 75 million barrels a day.

The 40 percent efficient transportation will use only about 30 million barrels per day to propel vehicles. With 70% efficiency, to provide 30 million barrels per day, the total of about 43 million barrels petroleum a day will be required. As petroleum constitutes about 60 percent of total petroleum used, the world should produce 43/60x100 = 71.7 million barrels a day, instead of 120 millions a day.

As of 2015, the world *conventional* (not total) oil production was around 70 million barrels a day. This is the plateau of conventional oil. If Peak Oil Production theory has any merit, it is reasonable to assume that oil production will stay on this plateau, with some fluctuations, till 2030.

Therefore, with 70 percent fuel efficiency, dependence on Middle East and other oil rich regions supply will remain as today for the foreseeable future. If combination of influencing factors don't change, we should expect the prices stay approximately the same as today, or higher, as it will take more energy to extract a unit of oil from the existing depleting deposits. The shale oil production will likely be reduced to insignificant quantity, although it will remain safety cushion in case of supply disruption.

There are some factors though, which may influence oil price dynamics in different ways.

Factors, pushing the price of oil down:

- Fuel cell engines can use natural gas and other substances for its fuel. This will reduce oil consumption for many applications, transportation including, further affecting supply side of equation
- Administrative measures to reduce traffic
- Reduction of vehicles weight by using lighter materials, thus diminishing fuel consumption
- Increased efficiency and volume of public transportation

Factors pushing the price up:

- Reduction of price of vehicle and traveling cost will significantly increase vehicle ownership
- Less expensive fuel will increase traveling distance, as has been the case so far
- Political disruption in the Middle East and Russia, which will result in resumption of shale oil production in the countries of its deposits
- General tendency of humanity use more energy to the maximum affordable at the time

To take these factors into account for predicting the future oil price, a sophisticated mathematical models are required. This subject is beyond the scope of this work.

To sum up, even in the best case scenario, dependency on supply of oil producing countries will remain almost the same as it is now. However, the price of oil will be higher, perhaps between $50 and $80 per barrel, subject to usual fluctuations and disruptions, so unpredictable for oil price.

Chapter 9. If Fuel Cell Technology is a Failure

Combination of technical, commercial and political problems slow the pace of fuel cell technology. Most likely it will not mature to mass production till 2030. Actually, some reputable forecasting agencies, like IEA and BP, do not take into account advancement of any particular technology, including fuel cell, as a factor of significance in their fossil fuel supply and demand forecasts. Thus, in terms of supply, the two primary factors will remain in force: conventional oil production and shale oil production. Others, such as renewables, will not reach the meaningful scale, as was discussed earlier.

IEA estimates that the U.S. shale boom will reach its plateau in 2020, and then will slow down till 2025. After that shale oil production will enter the phase of accelerated decline.

As technology of shale oil extraction is quickly improving, it stands to reason to assume that the average cost of shale oil in the U.S. will be between $60 and $70 per barrel till 2020, as it is now, in spite of shrinking pool of rich deposits. Another words, improving technology will offset the impact of depleting reserves. In the following years, when all best plays will have been processed, the low grade deposits become the only available option. This will be the point, at which the gap between demand and supply will be hard to fill. Fast growing world population, fast growing number of cars on roads, growth of energy consumption in China and India, will create new reality. Thus, even if the U.S. becomes self-sufficient and does not import oil, the existing sources of oil supply would not be able to satisfy the world's demand.

As was mentioned in the previous chapter, in 2030 world daily oil production will reach 120 million barrels per day. This is about 30 million barrels a day more than now.

In the recent past, the U.S. 4 million barrels a day of shale oil production pushed the oil price down from about $140 per barrel to less than $50 per barrel. In the total world production the shale oil output was slightly over 5 percent. But its affect on oil price was far greater that its share in the world oil supply.

The expected gap of 30 million barrels a day will certainly make much greater impact on oil price, but in the opposite direction.

The biggest share of oil consumption is the fuel produced to feed the continuously growing numbers of cars world wide. The growth is exponential, in line with other contemporary processes in technology and social life, and subjected to the law of compound interest. It took more than a century to reach 1 billion cars ownership worldwide. It will take about 15 years for this number to climb to 2.2 billion.

As any exponential growth, it will have a gradual affect, arguably in the first third of the period, approximately till 2020-2022. After that there will likely be a drastic spike of oil price, followed by a short plateau or slow increase, after which it will become a steady climb to new heights.

By 2020-2022 the U.S. shale oil production will no longer be a factor defining the total oil production and demand, as demand will increase by much more than their shale oil production of 4 – 5 million barrel per day. Then the oil price will jump at least to the height of pre-shale boom, which is about $140 per barrel. However, considering accelerated growth of China and India economy, as well as developing world, the likely price will be close to $200 per barrel.

The pattern of 2008 crisis will repeat: the economic growth of all countries around the globe will slow down. However, at this point no major disaster should be expected. There will be less demand for big cars and heavy vehicles, perhaps some decreased demand for cars world wide, higher prices for energy products and products made from petroleum. For sure it will prompt some administrative measures to save energy. Still, not the end of the world. However, after 2025 the picture will be different. The oil production plateau will end by that time and production will be on decline. The energy demand will increase much faster then in the preceding years, in line with accelerated population growth and the total world GDP growth. The price of oil will rise accordingly, perhaps to $600 or more per barrel in today's dollar value. If the price of oil is any indicator of what the price of gasoline would be, let's consider the following example.

In the middle of 2015 the oil price was around $50 per barrel.

Regular gasoline price in the U.S. was approximately $0.8 per liter.

With oil price jumping to $600 per barrel, the price of regular gasoline will rise to $9.6 per liter ($36.5 per gallon).

A trip of 100 kilometers would cost about $960. This is astronomical even for the well-to-do upper middle class.

Impact of high oil prices on aviation will be severe. Below is an approximate calculation of Boeing 747 return flight Toronto-Paris.

- As of August 2015, the price of aviation fuel is around $5.00 per gallon.

- The aircraft burns 1 gallon of fuel every second. The return flight Toronto-Paris lasts 14 hours and 10 minutes, which is 51,000 seconds.
- Considering average 500 passenger occupancy in economy class, the cost of fuel per passenger in today's economy is 51,000x$5:500= $510. The actual price of a ticket is about $1,900. Therefore, all expenses other than fuel are about $1,400.
- The price of aviation fuel in 2030 will jump to $50 per gallon – assuming it rises in pace with the price of oil
- The fuel cost for return flight Toronto-Paris per passenger will be 51,000 x $50/500 = $5,100. If we add to that the other existing expenses, the price of a ticket will be $5,100 + $1,400 = $6,500.

Even upper middle class won't afford such expense. It might remain an option for those who now travel business and first class. Their share in aviation industry revenue is about 27 percent. It is therefore reasonable to assume that aviation travel will shrink by about 70 percent.

If this happened, the majority of airports will be closed

The other consequences of high oil price:

I.   End of suburban life as we know it in North America and, to lesser extent, in Western Europe. Suburban life is supported only by the use of private cars. As the price of gasoline becomes beyond the means of middle class, people will have to move to the cities, closer to the place of employment, where a car will be used much less, or not at all.

II. A car will become an ultimate luxury item. The auto industry will shrink likely by 70-80 percent. Shrinkage of the auto industry will cause massive unemployment, as there are many other industries which depend on the auto industry.

III. Road building and maintenance will also shrink, along with the new suburban construction and maintenance. This will exacerbate unemployment further.

IV. Sharp increase in prices of agricultural products, as most fertilizers are manufactured from petroleum products. This will end food subsidies, food banks and food stamps, and all free niceties, invented by our society. As a large part of developed world societies depends on government subsistence, the outcome is predictable: unrest and massive criminal activity.

V. Private boat industry, private cottage industry, and vacation travel will shrink to the size affordable only to the upper class. This will further affect employment in negative way.

VI. Price of urban dwellings will skyrocket, as the existing space is not enough to accommodate the flood of suburban population.

VII. Unemployment will be slightly mitigated by moving outsourced industries back to the local production, as the cost of transporting goods by sea or air will be high enough to justify the local production.

VIII. Luxury items will be the thing of the past for most of population.

IX. There will be a sharp decrease of R&D funds because of drastically shrinking money supply and high inflation. This will mitigate the progress of technology.

Large U.S. volume of suburban defaults will inevitably cause a serious financial crisis. It will be much larger and longer than the real estate crisis in 2008, which was just the result of a speculative bubble, originated in the US. But in 2008, China came to the U.S. rescue, buying its government bonds, thus saving the dollar and the U.S. economy. This "rescue" came with the price: the U.S. federal debt skyrocketed to the unprecedented level and in 2015 it reached $18,5 trillion. During the suburban default between 2025 and 2030 (or a few years later), neither U.S. government, nor other government for that matter, would be able to save the dollar. All repercussions of such financial crisis is impossible to predict, although one point must be clear: it will be much more disastrous than any financial crisis the humanity has experienced so far. The only choice the governments would have is to print money. This will cause inflation large enough to make the government debt worthless. There will be no government subsidy on Medicare, education, welfare programs, police and all other vital services, without which the modern society cannot function. International financial obligations throughout the globe will cease to exist.

On international arena, international affairs will no longer be governed by the existing U.N. principles, whatever faults and deficiencies it has. All countries with vital energy resources will likely be under attack by military powers of the time.

There will be fragmentation of Middle East countries, whose population consists of different nationalities and religions. The most obvious case is Iran, Iraq, Syria, Lebanon, and some others.

Chapter 10. Environmental impacts.

So much has been said about pollution that it seems there is no need to say more. Although some scientific minds doubt that pollution affects the climate change, it is obvious that it does affect the health of biological life. So, what's the problem? Can't we just reduce pollution by substituting fossil burning technology with renewables? Is technical solution available, or not?

In theory, the technical solution is available. Although it is, at present, very expensive, it is also the question of preference: do we want to live in clean and healthy environment, and put up with a modest life style, or we want to sacrifice our health, and health of future generations, for endlessly increasing consumption?

The issue boils down to financial considerations. With the contemporary price structure of fossil fuel energy cost, one component is not taken into account: the cost of cleaning and storage of astronomical amount of poisonous waste thrown into atmosphere, soil and water. If it is included in the cost, the price of one kilowatt of energy would skyrocket.

Thus, as of 2003, according to World Coal Institute estimate, the capture and storage per tonne of carbon was $150-$200, and for CO_2 was $40-$60 per tonne. It was also stated in the report that the capture of billion tons of these poisonous substances makes this option uneconomic. In simple terms it means that we cannot afford cleaning coal pollution because energy production would become too costly. Further to the point, the cost of energy would cause considerable reduction of economic activity and income per family.

According to World Nuclear Association, burning coal produces almost 14 billion tonnes of carbon dioxide each year, which is released into atmosphere: most of this is from power generation. This is roughly 2.5 ton per every human. Every year. For every human. Could our ecological system recycle this waste?

This consideration is only for pollution at the place of coal burning. There are some other expenses, which supposed to be associated with the coal extraction and delivery to the power station: washing it and preparing it for transportation.

Also, the cost of coal energy does not include the cost of health care, which skyrockets not only in the areas of coal extraction, where it is the highest, but also far beyond, caused by poisoned underground waters, acid rains, dust, and some others.

But even as it stands now, the cost of renewable energy is approaching the cost of fossil fuel energy generation. Thus, according to EIA report of 2014, for energy plants entering service in 2018 the levelized cost (the per-megawatt cost - in real dollars - of building and operating a generating plant over an assumed financial life and duty cycle) will be as in the table 20 below.

Table 20. Levelized cost of energy generation by different technologies.

Plant type	Levelized cost $US
Geothermal	47.9
Natural Gas Advanced Combined Cycle	64.4
Wind	80.3
Hydro	84.5
Advanced Nuclear	96.1
Conventional coal	96.6
Biomass	102.6
Integrated Coal-Gassification Combined Cycle	115.9
Solar PV	130
Wind offshore	204.1
Solar Thermal	243.1

But renewables have a long way to go to be a dominant source of energy. There is not enough investment funds for such grandiose undertaking. There are too many technical and administrative obstacles, which slows substitution of combustion engines by electrical ones. It might take another 50-70 years for renewables to make a noticeable impact on transportation engine transformation and, in general, on energy generation.

Extensive research is underway to capture all harmful emission of the coal burning. Significant progress is achieved in this field. However, all existing power stations will work in the contemporary modus operandi in the foreseeable future. The choice of our domestic political life – and preference of the majority – live now, no matter what. For sure, politicians who would try to convince their constituencies that prudent, less affluent life is a wiser choice, do not have a chance to be elected.

Transportation, which includes cars, trucks, airplanes, ships and other vehicles, contributes globally about 15 percent manmade carbon dioxide. U.S. Department of Energy estimates that each vehicle emits 7-10 ton green house gases per year. Altogether it amounts to 1.7 billion tons of GHGs (Green House Gas) per year.

Although efficiency of cars is improving, mileage per vehicle is increasing, thus negating the effect of efficiency. Therefore, by 2030, when the number of cars worldwide will double, the combustion pollution will increase respectively, and reach approximately 3.5 billion tons.

So far, no administrative or taxation measure was effective enough to slow the pace of cars growth on the roads. But, as everything in real life, growth of things or occurrences is never endless: it has seeds of self-destruction, and these seeds suddenly become monsters at the time when the size of their environment reaches a critical mass.

If not for technology advancement, there will be two developments, the affect of which will wipe out most of the cars worldwide.

The first factor is the rise of oil price to $600 per barrel by 2030. As was demonstrated in the previous chapters, if not for technology breakthrough, this is inevitable. Most likely the vehicle fleet will shrink by 70-80 percent. When the number of cars is reduced to a few hundred millions, the problem with carbon dioxide will become less pressing then it is now.

The second development will be a drastic reduction in the number of people living on earth. This issue is analysed in depth in the last chapter. As it demonstrates, in the next 100-150 years the earth's population will shrink by 50 percent. This will result in reduction of everything produced and in operation, including the vehicle fleet. This is going to be a long-term trend, which will affect all biological life on the planet Earth.

Chapter 11. Short Term Oil Price Impact on International Affairs

For the Middle East oil-rich countries oil has been a primary instrument in their international policy and in domestic affairs. Of equal importance it is to Russia. The price of oil therefore affects the stability and perhaps the very existence of regimes in these countries. But their financial dependence on the price of oil varies. The common denominator is: at what price these countries balance their fiscal break-even budgets? The table 21 shows this budget-oil price relations as of 2014.

Table 21. Fiscal breakeven – the price of oil required to balance national budgets.

Country	$ per barrel
Abu Dhabi	55
Kuwait	61
Qatar	65
UAE	74
Russia	105
Iraq	105
Saudi Arabia	106
Oman	113
Bahrain	130
Iran	131
Algeria	131

This information is not meant to be accurate, but the difference from various sources is not significant for this discussion. As this table shows, major producers need the price of oil higher than $100 per barrel to balance their budgets. If the price is less, they have to use their currency and gold reserves to fill up the gap.

Unbalanced fiscal budget does not mean a disaster: a country could abandon its ambitious projects, or delay those which are not urgent, and still function, if it has sufficient cushion of international currency reserves to maintain the "break even crisis budget". This is to pay government workers salaries, maintenance of exiting infrastructure, minimum social services – another words, to maintain the status quo.

Break-even budgets of Russia and Iraq are close to their corresponding break-even crises budgets. Other oil producing countries will have to cut their expenses and use their budget surplus as long as the price of barrel is below their fiscal breakeven price.

As mentioned in previous chapters, the price of oil will not rise above $80 per barrel at least till 2020, most likely till 2025. It means that in 10 years even the richest oil producing countries will have no foreign currency reserves to balance their budgets.

With exception of Oman, all oil rich countries provide financial support, in various degree, to radical Islam groups and terrorist organizations. This is not necessarily the government support: rich individuals of these countries are big donors as well.

There are three prime factors in the Middle East, which are the source of hostility: religious confrontation of Sunni and Shia Muslim sects, widespread poverty in the region, and existence in the some countries a variety of ethnic groups, which have aspiration for independence.

It would be unrealistic to expect any compromise between them in the foreseeable future.

Sunni-Shia animosity goes many centuries back. There were times when it was dormant, or suppressed by dictatorial regimes. In the past, as it is at present, Muslim societies have demonstrated absence of tolerance to other people's beliefs or their way of life. As a result, almost all oil-rich Middle East countries participate in sectarian conflicts.

The direction of donor's country financial support therefore depends on its demographic and religious composition. Its brief overview is shown in Table 22.

Table 22. Religious sectarian composition of rich oil producing countries.

Country	petroleum in government revenue	religion	Industry	Population millions	Sponsor of
Kuwait	95%	70% Sunni, 30% Shia	Mostly oil related	3.4	ISIS
Qatar	70%	70% Wahhabi Muslims (Shia)	Almost all oil related	2.2	Hamas, other Shia groups
UAE	85%	85% Sunni, 15% Shia	diversified	9.4	Taliban, LeT, Al Qaeda, Hamas
Russia		Not applicable	diversified	143	All terrorist groups
Iraq	90%	51% Shia, 42% Sunni.	Mostly petroleum related	34	Fighting ground of factions
Saudi Arabia	Almost 100%	90% Sunni, 10% Shia	Almost all oil related	29	Taliban, Al Qaeda, ISIS
Oman	45%	70% Ibadi Muslims (Neither Shia no Sunni) Sunni 13% Shia 6%	Mostly oil/gas related	3.2	Against terror and fighting of any kind
Bahrain – governed by Sunni minority	70%	70% Shia, others are Sunni	Petroleum. Aluminum, finance, construction materials	1.4	ISIS
Iran	45%	90% Shia	Diversified industries	78	Hamas, Hezbollah, Al Qaeda, Islamic Jihad, Syrian regime

Oman is the only country among them which does not support terrorism: more so, it actually undertakes measures against terrorist activity of any radical sect both inside and outside the country. Its dominant religion is neither Sunni nor Shia. In consequence, the country has no interest in participating in any conflict in the region. Financially, Oman is better off than all: it does not depend on oil revenues as much as other oil producing countries, has huge currency reserves and, which is of utmost importance, has the government which proved in considerable length of time that it is capable of implementing prudent financial policy in bad and good times.

All donors of terrorism try to avoid sectarian fights inside their countries. They all delegate the trouble to their proxies outside their borders, and watch closely the balance of power: wars can quickly spill over their borders.

The main sponsors of terrorism are Iran and Saudi Arabia. Others take sides in accordance with their sectarian identity, as shown in the Table 17.

One may ask a question: if the price of oil will stay below $80 per barrel for long, would Muslim countries-sponsors of terrorism reduce or stop their financial support to warring factions in the Middle East? If so, would more peaceful mood settle in this region at the time of financial trouble?

The key to this question is to define the point of historical development stage of the Middle East Muslim world culture. As George Friedman said in his book "The Next 100 Years: A Forecast for the 21st Century," cultures live in three stages: Barbarism, Civilization and Decadence. According to Friedman, "Barbarians believe that the customs of their village are the laws of nature and that anyone who doesn't live the way they live is beneath contempt and requiring redemption or destruction." This is a laconic, but exact definition of barbarism, covering all its aspects. That is exactly the state the Muslim world lives in. Of course there is some influence of the Western culture on some of Muslim population. As Friedman put it, "Obviously all cultures contain people who are barbaric, civilized, or decadent, but each culture is dominated at different times by one principle." There is no doubt which principle dominates the Muslim world.

Western culture went through barbarism a few centuries ago. This was a period of wars, genocides, atrocities, and intolerance to any thought which was not in conformity with barbarism. This is exactly the period Muslim countries go through now. It will last long: not necessarily centuries, as social developments accelerate in modern times, but certainly well into the end of this century. There is no force, other than devastating war, similar to WWII, which would stop the bloodshed and reconcile the barbaric differences in this region. The most striking evidence is, that no financial difficulties or prosperities in the countries of this region had any influence on the mentality and bellicose stance of its people.

So far, oil price fluctuations, as well as financial difficulties in the Middle East have not diminished the sponsor's financial support, neither has it reduced the intensity of sectarian hatred.

A good demonstration of this point is Iran. It launched its massive support for terrorism in 1979, when clerics seized the power. At that time Iran was one of the poorest counties in the region. The war with Iraq from 1980 to 1988 strained all county's resources. And yet, Iran-sponsored terrorism proliferated in the region, and Iran's financial support never decreased or interrupted. Saudi Arabia, its most powerful foe, has no choice but to match its efforts to counter Iran's Shia proxies in their assault on Sunnis.

There is also evidence that Russia, the U.S. and Western Europe are getting involved in the Syrian civil war, providing military hardware and financial support to the factions of their choice. If history is any guide, the more players are drawn into the conflict, the longer it lasts, and the more threat to international stability it becomes.

In the sphere of international politics Iran's stance is the most radical and bellicose among the rest of Middle East countries. Islam, in Iran's clerics interpretation, must rule the world: this concept was expressed openly many times over and over again. However, a closer examination of their actions reveals that not all infidels are equals in the eyes of Ayatollahs. In the real world there are two large groups of infidels, which Islam must confront: Western civilization, which includes the U.S., Europe and Australia, and Oriental powers, the major of which are China and Japan.

Western civilization is tolerant to Islam as no other. Tolerance, and freedom of religion are cornerstones of democracy and constitutions of Western countries. There is no need to proof this with facts and arguments. But the stance of Oriental world toward Muslim religion is fundamentally different, if not hostile.

Here are a few facts relevant to Japan's attitude towards Islam followers:

- Obtaining immigration visa for a Muslim in Japan is virtually impossible
- Active promoters of Islam face deportation or jail sentence
- No courses exist who teach any Islamic language
- No collective Muslim gathering in streets or squares are allowed: fines are high, and deportation is an option

- No mention of Sharia law or halal food allowed

There are many other restrictions and regulations related to immigration, business and visiting visas, temporary living or settlement of Muslims in Japan. No need to mention them all. Did this policy inspire animosity of radical Islam against Japan?

Suffice it to say that there has been no single Japanese victim of Muslim terrorist attack in Japan. There was no registered case when an imam (there is only one in Tokyo) teaches intolerance to other people's beliefs, Jihad or any radical Islamic views in Japan, unlike it is in Europe, in the U.S. and in Canada.

There is another phenomena, worth a mention: Muslims inside Japan, and outside its borders, do not complain about discrimination of Muslims or their harassment. This is Japan, and one can cry his protests as long as he wants: no one would respond.

On diplomatic front Japan was trying to establish friendly relations with oil producing Muslim countries, without changing its attitude towards Islam inside Japan. Japan's concern is obviously oil supply. But this issue now is not much of importance, as the oil price will stay low for the time being and alternative sources of supply are easy to locate. For at least till 2025 Japan will not push hard to portray itself as a Muslim-friendly country.

China takes even a tougher stance against Islam. It introduced legislations against Muslims demands to prohibit selling of alcohol in public places, to impose a mandatory scarf for women, and others. Any attempts of Muslims to enforce the Islamic way of life on the local population is persecuted. There were, of course, some protests in the Muslim world and among liberally-minded activists in the West, but they did not last long. This is

China: it will do whatever it considers right, regardless if you cry or not. Actually, to be fair, China does not oppress Islam as a religion, as long as it is not aggressive. However, it responds in decisive, and often cruel manner to Muslim's demand to impose their way of life on other people.

China does not grant permanent citizenship to foreigners. Immigration to China does not exist, and therefore there will be no Muslim immigrants in China in foreseeable future.

China's well-being, as well as Japan's, is dependent on oil supply from oil-rich Muslim countries. The longer low oil prices exist, the less interested China would be to proof its tolerance towards unreasonable demands of Muslim devotees.

In spite of the Oriental world's intolerance to radical Islam on the one hand, and Western tolerance on the other, Iran proclaims over and over again that its main enemy is America. What is the matter? Is there any hole in the Iranian concept of the right and the wrong?

Hostility of Muslim religion toward the West is profound and deeply rooted. Western way of life is attractive to all Third World population, and Muslims are not an exception. With proliferation of communication technology and easy access to information, Western ideas and its way of life influence many: some emigrate to Western countries and America, and many among them adapted well to the predominantly Christian societies. There is nothing tangible that clerics have to offer to their people other than fanaticism, Jihad, and alienation from all that threatens the spiritual unity of Muslims and their subjugation to clerics. Peaceful coexistence with the West therefore is not possible in principle, as it eventually would destroy the foundation of this religion, and transform uncompromising postulates of Islam into something else. Oil price therefore, will not affect fundamentals of the existing Muslim stance in all aspects of international politics.

Chapter 12. Aspects of Middle East Politics

It may seem that confrontation line of the Muslim world in the Middle East is between Sunni and Shia. In reality, the Middle East is fragmented into ethnical groups, and within them into religious faiths. The force of animosity between ethnicities in the region is much stronger then the sense of religious identity, and counts many centuries back. It has been suppressed by dictatorial powers of the conquerors, and erupted at the moment when the strength of the ruler's grip was weakened by a few destabilizing factors:

- Russia's war in Afghanistan
- Unexpected wealth of oil-producing Gulf countries
- Influx of information and information technology from the industrialised world
- America and Western Europe interference, political, economical and military, in the Middle Eastern countries affairs
- Lately, chaos in the region was enhanced by Russian and American involvement in Syrian war
- Refugee flight from dangerous zones

Now we witness an extraordinary chaotic picture of turmoil in the region. The primary leaders of confrontation between Shia and Sunni are Iran and Saudi Arabia. Iran has an aspiration to be not only the Shia leader, but also the leader of the whole Muslim world.

Saudi Arabia, predominantly Sunni country, has no choice but to confront its opponent, thus in fact assuming the leadership role.

As both branches of the Muslim faith are still in barbaric stage, no reconciliation or peaceful co-existence is possible. History teaches us that the barbaric transition is not a short-term phase: it lasts centuries, until mentality and the way of life elevates society up to the next stage.

At present, the only imaginary condition of Muslim unity is a conquest of one religious sect of the other and exercise its power over it. This is not going to happen in the foreseeable future: if anything, neither America, no Russia would let it happen, albeit for different reasons. They have many instruments, including military intervention, which will destabilize a wanna-be hegemon from within and via their proxies from outside.

This is though a pure hypothetical assumption: there is no single country in the Middle East which possess military and economic power to unite the Muslim world.

Aside from realities, to which arguments this part of the globe is impervious, is there any spiritual goal, which cloud unite, even temporarily, Sunnis and Shias?

Iran offers two, which could be combined into one: death to America and death to Israel. Implicitly, the call is for death to Western civilization.

If death to Israel might look achievable due to its small size and population (but not necessarily realistic), the destruction of America by Iran, or by any improbable Muslim coalition, is totally absurd. Suffice to briefly review statistics of military hardware and personnel of American war machine – largely available on the Internet - to realise the futility of any military confrontation with it. However, for Muslims of the Middle East, who still live in the delusion of imam's propaganda, it might seem as a realistic and honourable goal.

In spite of delusions stemmed from propaganda and politics, the reality inevitably sets in. One thing is death wish, another is to devote resources and military to take action. Neither Sunnis no Shias are ready for such a fight, even united. In contemporary chaos of wars, economic hardships, influx of refugees, low oil and gas prices, which will likely stay until 2020, a serious unity against the 'common enemy' is beyond any assumption and probability.

All bellicose rhetoric of Muslim spiritual leaders can not change the fact that the primary division between people of this region is not that much a matter of faith as ethnicity. The table 23 shows ethnical and sectarian composition of the most important players in the Middle East policy. The numbers in this table are not meant to be accurate, and up to date. Neither they could be, as demographics in this region is changed almost daily. But they are good enough for the argument's sake.

Table 23. Ethnical and Religious composition of Middle East Muslim Countries.

Count	Pop. ml	Ethnic group	Mln.	% in pop.	religion	% in group
Iraq	32.5	Arabs	23.7	73	Shia Muslims	57%
					Sunni	18%
		Kurds	7.2	22	Sunni	20%
		Other	1.6	5		
Iran	77.5	Persian	47.3	61	Shia	98
		Azeri	12.4	16	Shia	98
		Kurds	7.8	10	Sunni	66
					Shia	27
					Other	7
		Other	10	13		
Syria	23	Arabs	20.9	90	Sunni	65
					Alawites (Shia)	13
					Christians	10
					Other	12
		Kurds	2.1	9	Sunni	76
					Other Muslims	24
		Other		1		
Turkey	77.7	Turks	58	75	Sunni	
		Kurds	15	18	Sunni	
		Other	6	7		
Jordan	8.0	Arabs		98	Sunni	97
Egypt	87	Egyptians (Arabs)			Sunni	90
Saudi Arabia	27.5	Arabs	24.8	90	Sunni	87
					Shia	13
		Other	2.7	10	Other	

All large ethnical groups in these countries have an aspiration for independence. Notably so are Kurds. As soon as any slack in the rope around their neck is detected, they stage war for the country of their own. This is the case in Iraq, and lately in Syria, when the dictatorial grip of the government lost its strength. The same problem is looming over Iran and Turkey. Kurds will be a problem for all countries where their presence is significant. Kurds live in the uninterrupted stretch of land, where they are a decisive majority. It is quite natural for them to have their own country on the territory that they own. As history demonstrates, for Kurds independence is the first priority, much more important than any Sunni-Shia confrontation.

Syria is a precursor of Kurds uprising elsewhere. Currently they are being armed and trained by America. Kurds are good fighters. Properly trained, they will pose a formidable force. Their victory in Syria and Iraq is just a matter of time. When it happens, Turkey and Iran will be alarmed.

Besides Kurds, Iran has another ethnical problem, which is becoming evident with the passing years: Azeris. This is a large, homogeneous group, making up to 16 percent of population. They have a common border with Azerbaijan – an independent state of Azeris. Spiritual unity with Azerbaijan, proximity to independent Azeri state, common language and identity are ever present factors, which inspire Iranian Azeri's wish to break away from Iran and unite with Azerbaijan. Considering barbarian mentality of Iranian government – as any government in this region for that matter – the disintegration of Iran is inevitable. Both Azeris, and Kurds will have a strong support from the US and likely from Russia and some other Arab countries.

When Kurds state is established on ruins of Iraq and Syria, Turks will be in a precarious position with their Kurds. Letting them go is out of the question: Turks aspiration for expansion or, it least, for increasing their sphere of influence, is unbending. International situation in Turkey is so complicated that any guess would be a wild fantasy, as there are too many social and political components, whose interactions are too complicated and make any prediction worthless.

This region is the place where three former empires have either common borders or close proximity: Turkey – the Ottoman Empire, Iran – Persian Empire, and Russia. Their history is a relentless fight with each other, and internal ethnical struggle for independence. All these empires had been in process of decay and disintegration, but this process is not finished yet. The proof if it is a remaining composition of ethnicities, which are not willing to live with each other in the same country.

When an empire rises, whatever it does, right, wrong or stupid, works eventually to its benefit and enhances its strength. But when the process of decay starts, it never stops, and the opposite logic is evident: no matter how clever and expedient decisions and actions of an empire are, they all add strength to forces of its decay.

There is not much that remains from former empires. Spanish empire became an insignificant Spain. Portugal empire became a small Portugal. Just England remains from the British empire. Turkey and Iran shrunk, but not to the minimum they are destined, as these states are a composition of different ethnic groups, which have the commonality of territory, language and customs.

Turkey and Iran remnants of empires are not going to be such in their contemporary formation. This has never been the case in history. History tells us that decay of an empire is an irreversible process. Further disintegration is on the cards.

There is one issue in the Middle East, which will forever be a sore spot for all its countries: the existence of Israel. Although the global unity of Sunnis and Shias against Israel is almost impossible in foreseeable future, a unity of Arab world is not out of reality. The only country which can unite Arabs against Israel is Egypt. Being an Arab country, and Muslim, and with common border with Israel, it is a much better candidate for Arab unity, albeit temporary, than a non-Arab Iran, or a non-Arab Turkey. But Egypt is very weak both economically and militarily. It will remain as such a few decades, until its population growth stops and begin shrinking. This would be the starting point of its rapid economic development.

If Egypt becomes a military power and decides to attack Israel, there will be no state that will help Israel in this war. Israel is the only country in this region, which the U.S. will not defend with its military force. The US 'friendship', as we witnessed in many occasions, is only the matter of expediency. From strategic point of view, Israel is a small component of its ever-changing global strategy.

Anyway, the major, a really bloody war for Israel is a few decades away, likely well into the second half of the 21st century.

To add some mystery to the issue, it is quite interesting to mention the prediction of Isaac Newton, the English genius in the field of physics and mathematics. His writings became the object of scrutiny only in the last 50 years, for reasons we will not discuss here. According to him, the Jewish messiah will come in the year 2060. May be not exactly the messiah, but something shuttering the world will come at the date. Who knows? After all, his prediction of a major cataclysm in 1940s had really come about. You never know how this genius had came to his conclusions.

The so called peace process between Arabs and Jews is the greater hoax and gibberish in history. Surprisingly, it fools only Jews. This happens perhaps because they do not have any experience with their own statehood, and also due to their belief that the world does not understand them and eventually will listen to reason. In fact, this conflict could not be resolved in a compromise for the following obvious reasons:

1. Israel is a land of dispute. Arabs claim that all this land is theirs. As history shows, land claims never die: they may be dormant, but never go away. Whether anyone of them is right or wrong does not matter: Jews have nowhere to go. They have no choice but defend themselves

2. Spiritual and religious differences between Arabs and Jews. Arabs are at the stage of development which excludes compromise. A consent to tolerate the Jews as their neighbours, with their contrasting flourishing state is an insult to Arab pride and mentality

3. Hostile attitude of the world towards Jews, providing great moral and financial support to Arabs in general and Palestinians in particular.

The conflict between Arabs and Jews is tiny if compared with contemporary international confrontations. If not for the Jews, it would pass with no publicity in the press. The size of the disputed land is close to nothing. The size of Israel is about 21,000 square kilometres. For comparison, lake Ontario in Canada is about 19,000 square kilometres, very close to the size of Israel. How many people know lake Ontario?

The value of this land, before Jews took the full control of it, was close to nothing: no natural resources, no arable land, no water, no anything. Conquering it does not justify the means to do so. And yet, any small skirmish where Israel is involved is the hottest subject of international press. Any war with Israel, where casualties just a few hundreds – almost nothing in comparison with

106

other conflicts in the Middle East, counting hundreds of thousands deaths and many millions refugees – cause all international media to flock to the Palestinian conflict zone.

Tens of millions refugees around the globe have been settled. As of 2015, 60 million displaced persons have been registered. Not much of a concern to the UN. But, according to international conventions, descendants of refugees are not considered refugees... except Palestinians, displaced by Israeli conflict in 1948 and in 1967. Majority of the UN resolutions are related to Arab-Jewish conflict. The list is endless. The point is, that Israel – Palestinian conflict is much more than a land dispute and refugees. Its roots are of international, spiritual character, and only millenniums can change it, if at all. This is the ground for the long-lasting peace between Arabs and Jews.

In spite of the obvious absurdity of the situation, most of the UN activity is around this conflict. America, Russia and Western Europe are involved in the so-called piece process. Most academia of the Western world is passionately anti-Israel, demonstrating total disregard to logic and facts. This combination of factors is going to last until really disastrous conflicts will erupt around the globe.

Chapter 13. The Future of Russia and its Policy

Russian policy is deeply rooted in its history of the last few centuries. In a nutshell, it has two distinguished features: relentless effort to expand its territories or sphere of influence on international arena, and oppression of its population.

All empires had expansionists policy, but they had clear reasons for that: to plunder the foreign population, impose taxation on them, or eliminate possible enemy, if the bordering country was gaining strength and might be a threat. As the history of the last hundred years demonstrates, Russia had no economical benefits from its expansion. Particularly after the WWII, it was for dominance and influence for its own sake.

There were a few short periods when Russia's aspiration for expansion was dormant. The last such period was in 1990s, when Yeltsin was in power. After his successor took the helm, we witness a rapid revitalising of this policy. Annexation of Crimea, war with Georgia, Ukraine, and escalation of tension with other neighbours are a vivid proof of it.

This policy was accompanied by spreading poverty among Russian population. But the paradox is that the majority of Russian population has always supported the rulers of the country in their bloody endeavours. At present, we witness the same phenomena: the majority of population supports the government in its adventures. What is the secret of this unity?

Through all its history Russian rulers brainwashed their people into thinking that Russians are the greatest and the best. It was suffice to be Russian to qualify for superiority over any other national. Although poverty has always been widespread, and inability of the country to develop a meaningful economy and improve living conditions was obvious, the notion of Russian superiority was unshakable. And so was the harmony of the public mood and the government policy.

The whole economy, ineffective as it had been, collapsed with the fall of the Soviet Union. Only a few industries survived and later improved: oil and gas, mining and military production.

Years of high fossil fuel prices were a period of Russia's relative prosperity. But the well-being of population was solely dependent on oil and gas revenues. During this period Russia did not develop a substantial domestic industry. Most of food items and virtually all consumers products were supplied by import.

Russia intensified its expansionists policy at the least favourable time for it: oil prices plunged in 2014 below Russia's break-even fiscal budget level.

Now Russia is back to its historic basics: worsening poverty of its population, shrinking public service, and massive brainwashing assault on the public, with its never failed component of Russian superiority. Its other premises are:

- Russia's enemies are America and Western Europe, and all democratic countries. They contemplate a war against Russia
- Ukraine and some other countries, members of the former Soviet Union, are enemies as well. They intend to unite with NATO in its aggression against Russia
- Russia has military might capable of defeating any enemy, be it NATO, America, or both.

In essence, Russian ruler's hostility towards America and Western Europe has the same foundation as it was at the time of the Soviet Union: the country's inability to provide a similar economic and social prosperity.

The most progressive Russians, who are considered as dissidents or traitors at different times, ask the same question over and over again: how come that Russia, the richest country in the world by territory and resources, remains one of the poorest countries in Europe?

With proliferation of communication and information technology, inability of Russian government to develop economy was no longer a secret. Similar to the situation in Muslim countries, the very existence of Western democracies and their way of life is a threat to those, who usurp power in Russia. But since the government and the Russian majority formed a solid unity, it is reasonable to expect that this centuries-old policy will continue until such time when the whole economy will collapse, and the government will not be able to function. It may sound unrealistic to expect, but the first signs of it already show up.

The most convincing evidence of contemporary government financial abyss is its lease of some Siberian territory to China for the period of 49 years. This step was unthinkable in the past history of Russia. In fact, China has no intention to leave this territory ever. The leased territory is many times greater than Crimea. Its lease signifies defeat of Russian policy in the Far East, and Russia's desperate need for money and Chinese support. It tells more than numbers that deterioration of Russia may not be the matter of too distant future.

There are a few trends in this country, which continue, in accelerated pace, with the passing years:

- Flight of capital from Russia
- Constant emigration, most part of it is professionals with higher education
- High mortality rate, low fertility rate, and negative population growth
- Diminishing capital investment into industries
- Deterioration of the nation's physical and mental health

And host of others.

The only way to stop deterioration of the country is introduction of profound structural reforms, but this will never happen, as it means the end of power of those who usurped it.

Along with acute shortage of oil revenues, continuous deterioration of all branches of industries, and deepening poverty of population, Russia will intensify its aggressive stand against its neighbours and Western democracies. It will side with and support the most oppressive regimes all over the world, and will do whatever it can to harm Western interest.

When the price of oil jumps to $600 per barrel, the situation in Russia will improve, albeit temporarily. This price of oil will result in a severe world wide crises, which will affect all countries without exception.

Some aspects of Russian international policy are not so illogical as they might seem. They act not only out of desire to reach its former glory. The root of it is a geopolitical probability of different scenarios. Any such consideration is based on an assumption: *what if*?

So *what if* the Western Europe gets back to its aggressive stand and moves against Russia in an attempt to acquire its vast resources? *What if* Ukraine invites the

US or NATO military force to its territory, which is a few hundred kilometres from Moscow? *What if* Turks decide to move north, to take over Caucasus? *What if* Iran decides to take over Azerbaijan? There are many *what ifs*. None of them, from geopolitical point of view, should be ignored.

Historically, the Russian important defence from invasion was its territorial depth. Now it shrunk from more than thousand kilometres to a few hundreds. It is going to shrink even further, as logic of a decaying empire suggests. In geopolitics no friendships or trust has a place. It also has no place for morality or justice. Reality replaces them all.

What if strategic thinking is not just a property of empires and strong states. It is also a component of smaller states' policy, whose existence depends on their affiliation with stronger states or blocks. Naturally, all Russian neighbours, who were under the dictatorship of the former Soviet Union, think the same way, but from different perspective: *what if* Russia moves in, to subjugate them again? Nothing could be worse for them than that. Their only hope is to get support from NATO and America. So, it is quite obvious that once the process of mistrust and stand-off has started, it never gets in reverse gear. The cataclysm will materialise sooner or later: it could me a military clash, similar to World War II, or a peaceful collapse of Russia, as it was as a result of the First Cold War at the end of twentieth century. But a some sort of resolution is inevitable.

Now Russia faces tough choices. If the right decision is theoretically possible at all in this situation, it takes a clever government to take it and overcome obstacles in the most expedient way. But Russia does not have such government, and has no chance to have it, as I argued in my monograph "Putin, the Russian Elite, and the Future of Russia."

We live in an interesting time, which can be labelled as *A Turning Point of History*.

Chapter 14. Distant Future of Humanity

What awaits humanity in the next hundred years? Although none of the contemporary generations would live that long, some of them will witness and recognize the new trends as they age. To understand social dynamics and its possible outcomes, it is not suffice to identify and predict the progress of technology. Of no less, or perhaps even of greater importance, are demographic trends. They all are interconnected, and the outcome of their interaction is a new trend, which is already traceable and could be extrapolated into the future.

Scholarly understanding of demographics, and its correlation with technology, have undergone considerable transformation in the last 150 years. However, judging by contemporary forecasts, it is still under influence of Malthusian theory, whose ground was laid out by Thomas Malthus (1766-1834). Its essence is the concept that population grows is faster than food supply. This inevitably brings into play the nature's mechanisms of equilibrium: epidemics, wars, famine, and other possible 'positive' (as Malthus had put it) factors, which reduce the population to match the food supply.

In essence, this was not so much a theory as an observation of facts and trends, projected into the future. Indeed, up to twentieth century this was a mechanism, which regulated human population growth. In general, this is the way the nature balances population of any species in animal kingdom. However, in the twentieth century the pattern of demographics had changed, defying the nature's mechanism, as shown in the table 18 below.

Table 24. World Population Growth

Year	millions
1700	682
1750	791
1800	978
1850	1,262
1900	1,650
1950	2,561
1999	5,978
2008	6,707
2014	7,215

Population growth since 1950s was exponential. Progress in agricultural technology and medicine led to increased food production, which growth was as fast, or even faster, than the population growth. But, at the same time, other forces and trends came into play, which carry with them the gene of destruction.

This is not a sci-fi fantasy: in the following discussion this notion will be supported by statistics and logical relations between cause and effect.

In the previous history of humanity, the population growth, along with the improved food supply, was attributed to fertility rate. The more kids a family could afford to feed, the more kids they produced. The limit was only a woman's fertility rate, which is the number of children born per woman during her childbearing years.

No knowledge of mathematics is required to understand that at least two children per family are required to replace the parents and maintain the same number of people in a society. In reality, a fraction more than 2 children is needed for the same purpose, as different ailments cause mortality among the new-born, illness affecting fertility of new generations, etc.

In the last 50-60 years statistics shows that two demographics trends have developed, which had no precedent in the previous history of humanity: diminishing fertility rate, which supposed to slow or stop the population growth, and actual fast population growth. This looks like a puzzle: these two trends should not co-exist with each other. But in reality they work together.

If looked through the lenses of Malthusian theory, humanity entered the era of paradox: the better off a country, the less is its population fertility rate. Another words, the more food and better quality of life a family could get, the less is a number of children they are willing to raise. The table 25 demonstrated this, showing statistics of born children per woman in the some populous countries (excluding India).

Table 25. Children born per woman in 2014

County	Births per woman
US	2.01
Australia	1.77
Russia	1.61
China	1.55
Germany	1.43
Italy	1.42
Japan	1.4
South Korea	1.25
Hong Kong	1.17
Singapore	0.8

The average number for all Europe (West and East) and Russia is roughly 1.6. Slightly larger is this number in poor countries, but nonetheless their fertility rate is quickly diminishing. What was the cause? After all, living conditions now are much better than in any time in the past.

There are a few interrelated factors. The most important one is accelerated urbanization in almost all countries in the world. As a UN report stated, "The urban population of the world has grown rapidly since 1950, from 746 million to 3.9 billion in 2014." This means that "In 1950, 70 percent of people worldwide lived in rural settlements and 30 percent in urban settlements. In 2014, 54 percent of the worldwide population is urban."

With urbanization, the following factors came into play.

- Living space in cities is expensive, and overall conditions are not conducive to large families
- Growing children is expensive. Most people decide to improve their living conditions rather than have many children
- In rural areas in the past, having big family made sense: kids took care of their parents when they get old and helpless. When kids were in their infancy and in adolescent years, they were a work force, which helped their families with agricultural activity. In the city this is no longer a consideration
- More people get college and higher education. Couples postpone the birth of their first child until after the education is completed, and often for a later date. The time span when a woman can get children shortens
- People born in educated family tend to get college and higher education as well, this way joining the population with low fertility rate

- Women have different psychological disposition in urban areas. Most of them chose not be a slave to their kids and family, but rather opt to have education, career, and better quality of life.

Urbanization is irreversible trend all over the globe. It goes in parallel with increased income per family, growing productivity in agriculture and, with it, low fertility rate.

Another factor is improved quality of life due to technological advances. Because of it, life expectancy is on the rise. Although new generations come with diminishing numbers due to lower fertility rate, older generation live longer, this way affecting population growth. This is the primary cause of population growth in the last few decades.

To understand the actual affect of diminishing fertility rate and aging population on demographics, let us consider a fictitious situation: a small country demographics, in which fertility rate is 1, which means one child per family.

For the sake of simplicity, I present an imaginary Happy Planet Republic. It starts its life with 16 couples, total 32 people, all aged 25. Their fertility rate is 1. Its generation structure is shown in Table. 26.

Table 26. Happy Planet Republic – start

Generation	Age	Number of people	Total	Comment
1	25	32	32	First generation

Its demographics will progress under the following assumptions:

- A woman's reproduction years are from 25 to 50, which is statistically true for a one-child family.
- Life expectancy is 75 years. Although more people will be older than that, their number does not affect reproduction years, and therefore has no affect on how many people are born from the following generations. Therefore, in long term the outcome will be the same.

Twenty five years later, the second generation is born. The demographics of the Republic is presented in Table 27.

Table 27. Happy Planet Republic – 25 years later

Generation	Age	Number	Total	Comment
1	26	32		16 couples
2	1	16	48	Population increased

The second row shows that 16 children were produced by 16 couples. The first generation consist of 32 people, the second generation of 16 people, altogether there were 48 people.

50 years later (25 years after the second generation was born) – the third generation was born (table 28). This change is shown in table 28.

Table 28. Happy Planet Republic – 50 years later

Generation	Age	Number	Total	Comment
1	51	32		First generation
2	26	16		8 couples
3	1	8	56	Further growth

In the table 28, there are 32 people 51 years old, who started the Happy Planet republic. There are 16 people of the second generation, and 8 people from the third generation. The Planet grew to 56 people. Then, the cumulative affect of low fertility rate and aging population takes place. After another 25 years, 75 years after the Planet has started, the 4th generation is born. The Planet population suddenly drops the first time, as shown in table 29.

Table 29. Happy Planet Republic – 75 years later.

Generation	Age	Number	Total	Comment
1	76	0		Starters – no one lives
2	51	16		8 couples
3	26	8		4 couples
4	1	4	28	Drop 50%

In the table 29, the first generation, older than 75 years of age, disappeared according to the assumption that the life expectancy is 75 years. After initial robust population growth in the Happy Planet Republic, there is a sudden drop of 50 percent in the number of living people. The planet is now populated only by the second generation, which is 16 people, third generation, which is 8 people, and the forth generation, which is 4 people, born by 4 couples (8 people) of the third generation.

After 25 more years elapse (100 years after the Planet had started), the second generation reaches 76 years, and therefore will no longer be living. The total population of the planet will be as shown in Table 30.

Table 30. Planet Population 100 later.

Generation	Age	Number	Total	Comment
2	76	0		Second generation
3	51	8		Third generation
4	26	4		Forth generation
5	1	2	14	Drop 50% from previous

As the Table 30 shows, the second generation is dead, therefore its number is zero.

The third generation is now 51 years old, and its number is 8. The fourth generation counts 4 people, and the fifth generation is only 2 people. The total living people on the Planet now is 14. There is a further 50 percent drop in the number of leaving people on the Happy Planet.

Another 25 years elapse, 125 years after the planet had started (Table 31).

Table 31. Planet 25 years later – 6th generation

Generation	Age	Number	Total	Comment
3	76	0		Third generation
4	51	4		Fourth generation
5	26	2		Fifth generation
6	1	1	7	Drop 50% from the previous

The third generation (Table 31) is now dead. Its number is zero. There are 4 people living from the fourth generation, two people from the fifth generation, and one from the sixth generation. Again, 50 percent drop in population number.

This is the end of Happy Planet Republic. Although 7 people are still alive, there is no further reproduction possible, and therefore no generation replacement. In fact, the end of population in this republic would come much sooner, because in order to maintain infrastructure of manufacturing, healthcare, law and order, and other industries and services, some minimum population is required. When one of economy component is reduced to zero, the whole society would plunge into chaos, which will enhance acceleration rate of mortality and degeneration of all society.

I would call such population dynamics as "gerontology fertility law." After a short period of rapid growth, in each following period of 25 years the population of Happy Planet shrinks 50 percent.

Even more interesting is to consider the actual numbers of the countries, whose population growth is rather typical demonstration of the *gerontology fertility law*. Japan is a good example, as the trend there is well established, and the first period of population meteoric growth has ended. Contemporary Japan's fertility rate is 1.4. It is not the lowest in the region, but not the highest as well. Table 32 shows Japan's demographics as of year 2014.

Table 32. Japan population 2014.

Age group	Male	female	total
0-14 years	8,681,728	8,132,809	16,814,537
15-24	6,429,429	5,890,991	12,320,420
25-54	23,953,643	24,449,655	48,403,298
55-64	8,413,872	8,400,953	16,814,825
65 years and over	14,218,655	18,531,653	32,750,308
Total			127,103,388

In further discussion the assumption is the same as for the Happy Planet Republic: the average age of delivering a child is 25. Although in reality the number of births will be spread over the period from 25 to 50 years of age, the final number after the end of the period should be the same. For simplicity, the table 32 was re-arranged into the table 33.

The actual coefficient of growth for fertility 1.4 is applied to women only, which is roughly half of population. This is about 0.7, if applied to the whole population.

Table 33. Japan population by age group

Genera tion	Age	Number	Total	Comment
1	50-75	53,150,562		43% of population
2	25-50	41,726,981		
3	0-25	29,134,957	124,012,500	

25 years later, Japan population will change as shown in the table 34.

Table 34. Japan Population 25 years later

Generat ion	Age	Number	Total	Comment
1	75+	0		
2	50-75	41,726,981		46% of population
3	25-50	29,134,957		
4	0-25	20,394,470	91,256,408	

In another 25 year, 50 years from now, Japan population will be as in Table 35.

Table 35. Japan Population 50 years later

Generation	Age	Number	Total	Comment
2	75+	0		
3	50-75	29,134,957		
4	25-50	20,394,470		
5	0-25	14,276,129	63,805,556	Population shrinks 50%

Then, 75 years from now:

Table 36. Japan Population 75 years later

Generation	Age	Number	Total	Comment
3	75+	0		
4	50-75	20,394,470		
5	25-50	14,276,129		
6	0-25	9,993,290	44,663,889	Population shrunk to one third

Then, 100 from now:

Table 37. Japan Population 100 years later

Generation	Age	Number	Total	Comment
4	75+	0		
5	50-75	14,276,129		
6	25-50	9,993,290		
7	0-25	6,995,503	31,264,922	Population shrunk to 1/4

With the existing fertility rate, which likely remains the same or lower in the foreseeable future, in hundred

125

years Japan will have just 25% of the contemporary population. In reality, population negative growth will accelerate, as fertility rate inevitably will reach 1.0 or lower, as it is now in some of Japan's neighbours.

What will happen with the white population over the globe? The interest is not a simple curiosity. According to statistics, this race will be in the vanguard of those whose population grows conforms to *gerontology fertility law*.

Contemporary white population in the world is approximately 1 billion. Its fertility rate is approximately the same as in Japan, 1.4 per woman. The following numbers are a very rough approximation, but they are not meant to be the basis of an accurate forecast. Rather, they demonstrate the trend, and the final calculation does not differ much from the ones which use complex mathematical models.

Here is the dynamics of the white race demographics – Table 38:

Table 38. White Population in Year 2015

Generation	Age	Mln.	Total mln.
1	50-75	460	
2	26-50	322	
3	0-25	218	1,000

Table 39. White Population 25 years later – Year 2040

Genera tion	Age	Mln.	Total mln.
1	75+	0	
2	50-75	322	
3	26-50	218	
4	0-25	153	693

Table 40. White Population 50 years later – Year 2065

Generation	Age	Mln.	Total mln.
2	75+	0	
3	50-75	218	
4	26-50	153	
5	0-25	107	478

Table 41. White Population 75 years later – Year 2090

Generation	Age	Mln.	Total mln.
3	75+	0	
4	50-75	153	
5	26-50	107	
6	0-25	75	335

Table 42. White Population 100 years later – Year 2115

Generation	Age	Mln.	Total mln.
4	75+	0	
5	26-50	107	
5	26-50	75	
6	0-25	53	235

The rest of the world will fair better, but not much. Urbanisation in all developing countries quickens its pace. Its current average fertility rate is just above 2. Therefore, the consequences for them will be similar to that of white race and Asian countries in Far East, such as Japan, China, Singapore, and others. The only difference is timing.

***

New trends in social life of affluent societies are precursors of the future upheavals. This has always been the case with new trends: whatever starts as a positive development, meant to improve quality of human life, turns out to be the cause of horrendous disaster. In the past, the primary goal of humanity was obtaining maximum food supply. But, as Ian Morris mentioned in his wonderful book "*Why the West Rules-for Now: The Patterns of History, and What They Reveal About the Future*", when food supply grew, so did the human population of the society which achieved prosperity. In line with this grew the number of rats and mice feeding on waste, as well as viruses and bacteria, harmful to human health. Inevitably epidemics erupted, wiping out the majority of population.

Now, food production and supply is no longer a concern of an individual in the developed world. Its modern societies have enough technology and power to produce as much food as a society wants, and even more. Our medical science and its applications eliminated the risk of epidemics.

Our understanding of poverty and financial hardships has changed beyond imagination of previous generations, and more so in the eyes of really poor nations, who know better what struggle for survival and hardships mean. A very good explanation of contemporary "poverty" in the US is in the article "Understanding Poverty in the United States: Surprising Facts About American's Poor" by Robert Factor and Rachel Sheffield. (Sep. 13, 2014, in The Heritage Foundation).

According to the Census Bureau, a record of 46.2 million persons in America were poor in 2010. "In most years for the past two decades, the Census Bureau has declared that at least 35 million Americans lived in poverty." The numbers may make an impression that America is in the category of poorest countries in the world. The authors though did a thorough work in defining what it means to be poor in America. Below is the summary of living conditions of American's poor.

- 80 percent of poor households have air conditioning. In 1970, only 36 percent of the entire U.S. population enjoyed air conditioning.
- 92 percent of poor households have a microwave
- Nearly three-fourths have cable or satellite TV
- Two-thirds have at least one DVD player, and 70 percent have a VCR
- Half have a personal computer, and one in seven have two or more computers
- More than half of poor families with children have a video game system, such as and Xbox or PlayStation
- 43 percent have internet access
- One-third have a wide-screen plasma or LCD TV

Close to 90 percent of poor families reported that there was never a shortage of food, clothing and other bare necessities.

There are many other interesting facts and conclusions in this article. No need to mention them all: the point is, that the notion of "hardship" and "poverty" has changed to something completely different. If in the past they meant deprivation of food, clothing and minimal shelter, now the basis of poverty definition is a comparison of living condition of a particular income category with the wealthy.

How American poverty compares with other countries?

According to UN Census, the average space per person in 2009 in America was 829 square feet (77 square meters). In "poor" households it was 515 square feet (48 square meters) per person.

In Russia, the average space per person for all population is 237 square feet (22 square meters) per person. Russia was chosen for comparison because it is not exactly a third world country, but still not a developed country by any standard.

Statistics on living space of "poor" category in Russia is hard to obtain. But the above mentioned statistics is sufficient to illustrate the point. America's "poor" person has 2.5 times more living space than the Russian average – not poor - person. We should assume therefore that an average Russian, by American standard, lives below the poverty line. However, the Russian population does not consider itself poor: a family of 4, having living space greater than 1000 square feet (93 square meters) considers itself fairly well-off.

In general, all conditions and concerns of survival, facing previous generations, are now removed from the daily life of modern affluent society. Care for children, care for elderly, even the care for an individual's health now in greater part is the function and burden of society and its social services. So, the struggle of individuals for physical survival is over. There is no "survival of the fittest" rule: every one survives, the strong and the weak, clever and not so. Does it create a new notion of reality in new generations? If so, what are the trends? Here they are.

Adult children live with their parents.

Interesting facts about this phenomena are in the article of Jordan Weismann, In "State" – a blog about business economy: "Why Do So Many Millenians Live with Their Parents? Two Theories: Marriage and Debt".

In 2014, according to the Census Bureau, 15% of 25-to-34 old Americans live with their parents. There is no shortage of attempts to explain this phenomenon. The most popular among them are these: delayed marriage, rising student's debts and unemployment. But there are adults who do not have a student debt, but still live with parents. The same author points out that "...living-at-home rates actually grew faster during the recession for young adults who never attended college than those who did."

Consideration of economy is the easiest cause to point out. However, financial difficulties had been much more severe and widespread among previous generations. The root, therefore must be in mental disposition and social notions, which sets apart the contemporary society from the previous ones. It is a systemic interaction of economic and social factors, which creates new mentality in the affluent society.

The simple fact is that living with parents was not an option in the past, but an easy choice at present. In the article of February 26, 2014, American Enterprise Institute, Mark J. Perry gives the following statistics, confirming this statement:

- Over the last 40 years , the average home has increased in size by more than 1000 square feet [100 sq. meters], from an average size of 1,660 square feet in 1973 to 2,679 square feet last year [2013].

- Meanwhile, the average household size has been declining, from 3.01 persons per household on average in 1973 to a new record low of 2.54 persons per household last year.

The author concluded that "... the average amount of living space per person in a new home has almost doubled in just the last 40 years – that's pretty amazing."

The primary socio-economic reason why young adults live with parents therefore is affordability. Why struggle, if the living space is available for free? Why marry, to share expenses with a spouse, if good living conditions are available without an effort to obtain them?

In the literature of social studies the trends of growing consumption, be it living space, food or luxury items, is considered as positive trends in affluent societies. But statistics hides a harmful psychological impact of availability of necessities on all society. It won't go away even if (and when), the living conditions worsen due to energy crisis or other possible events.

Single-occupancy household.

There is another interesting trend, well-presented in the Fortune article (Solo Nation: American Consumers Stay Single, by Eric Klinenberg): American nation quickly moves to a single occupant household.

In Jan. 2012, "Only 51% of adults today are married... and 28% of all households now consists of just one person – the highest level in U.S. history."

Particularly strong this trend is in big cities in the developed world. Further in this article, "Today more than 40% of households have just one occupant in cities such as Atlanta, Washington, DC,...this rate is similar in London and Paris, and even higher – a staggering 60% - in Stockholm."

The single household occupants is a category located on the other end of the spectrum, being opposite to those who live with their parents. They are employed, have a good income and live affluent, often intense social life.

As the above mentioned article states, "Their average per capita annual expenditure was \$34,471 in 2010, ... compared with \$23,179 per person in the highest-spending families with children."

Is this trend good for society? One point is clear: it speeds up the trend of decreasing fertility rate, pushing it down to one or none per woman. It also changes psychology and mentality of society, but its other behavioural consequences are not obvious at the time of this writing.

Increasing number of the mentally ill

This trend is an obvious socio-economic phenomenon. The better are the living conditions, the more mental illness is widespread. For instance, according to Anxiety and Depression Association of America (Facts and Statistics) "Anxiety disorders are the **most common mental illness in the U.S.**, affecting 40 million adults in the United States age 18 and older (18% of the U.S. population)."

If the current tempo persists, the mental illness will reach epidemic worse than plague of cholera. The difference is though that cholera disappears at some point even without medication, but mental illness is not. It is hard to treat, total recovery is hardly possible. It takes its debilitating toll on work force, health system, and a society as a whole.

Single Parenthood

In the U.S., unmarried births rate among blacks jumped from 20% to 72%. Among whites from 2% to 36%, and in all groups from 3% to 41%. (National Center for Health Statistics). Similar trends recorded in other developed countries, and, in lesser extend, in the countries of developing world. As most single-parents are mothers with low income, poverty and lack of care are obvious circumstances that affect psychological and physical development of a child. Academic achievements in school, as studies suggest, is lower, and obtaining collage and university education is a remote possibility. The study shows that income level affects academic performance stronger than single-parenting, but the fact is that majority of single parents are mothers (83% in the U.S.) with a low income, often far below the poverty line.

According to EducationNext (by Kathleen M. Ziol-Guest, Greg J. Duncan and Ariel Kalil) schooling completed from two-parent family in 2008 is above 35 percent, whereas from a single-parent family is below 25 percent. Even greater difference is the rate of collage completion: close to 40 percent for a two-parent family and below 10 percent for a single-parent family.

Since the time of this report, situation got worse. The point is that increase in the number of a single-parent family means the growing number of people living in poverty. Poverty breed poverty, affects educational level of a child, and leads to ant-social behaviour of those who gets deprived from a proper family environment.

Interesting data is provided in The New York Times (by Sam Dillion, Oct. 8, 2009)

- High school dropouts are 72 percent more likely to be unemployed as compared to high school graduates
- Nearly 80 percent of individuals in prison do not have a high school diploma

Decreasing demand for low-skill workers and ever-increasing number of school dropouts leads to higher unemployment and incarceration rate. In the same above mentioned article "...the collective cost to the nation over the working life of each high school dropout at $292,000."

According to Frontline publication "Among dropouts between the ages of 16 and 24, incarceration rates were a whopping 63 times higher than among college graduates."

Plenty of statistics is available on harmful consequences of single parenthood on the future of a child. But single parenthood rise is just one of social trends, traced in modern societies. It develops in close relations with other problems, thus affecting each other in an intricate way. Other developed countries have a similar trend. It progresses in parallel with accelerated proliferation of automation, robotics, and increased efficiency of production and service. If the trend continues, the crises, which magnitude is hard to predict, will take place in 2030. It will be caused by hundreds of million people, whom nobody needs and who have no place in the normal civilian life.

Biological deterioration of human race.

Robert Martin presents in his very interesting and informative book "How We Do It: The Evolution and Future of Human Reproduction" a summary of reproduction scientific studies around the globe. There are a few trends, which have clearly been identified.

- There is a convincing evidence of declining human sperm count. There is a certain minimum, below which a human reproduction is not possible. But even the count above minimum must be high enough to ensure a healthy reproduction. The author stated that as a result of diminishing sperm count, "it has become increasingly difficult to find sperm

135

donors who meet the criteria set by fertility clinics. Himov-Kochran and her colleagues concluded that this rapid deterioration of semen quality among fertile semen donors may shut down sperm donation programs." This goes parallel with other trends, which further exacerbate biological health of humanity: "Even more alarmingly, decreasing sperm count seem to have been paralleled by increasingly frequent abnormalities of the male reproductive system, including cryptorchidism, penis malformation, and testicular cancer."

- Artificial insemination became another cause of human biological degradation. Martin quoted another source that "...more than 3.5 million babies had been born world wide between 1978 and 2008 using IVF and related methods of assisted reproduction." The consequences were far from being a pleasant surprise. "Multiple births have occurred in about one in four pregnancies, compared with only one in almost a hundred births resulting from natural conceptions. Moreover, more IVF babies are born prematurely, and perinatal mortality is almost 2 percent, double that for controls. ... In a large-scale study of more than 60,000 births in Ontariom Darine El-Chaar at the University of Ottawa found that the risk of birth defects for babies born through IVF was about 60 percent higher than for those born after natural conception."

- A new trend was recorder in the US: a steep increase in the death rate of middle-aged Americans. According to Washington Post article of Nov. 3, 2015, it hits mostly white men and women ages 45-54 with less than a college education. As the author Joel Achenback put it, "An increase in the mortality rate for any large group in an advanced nation has been virtually unheard of in recent decades, with the exception of Russian men after the collapse of the Soviet Union."

In the same article, Jonathan Skinner, a professor of economics at Dartmouth College, sais: "High school graduates and high school dropouts are 40 percent of the population...... It's not just the 10 percent who didn't finish high school. It's a much bigger group." The scientists explain that "...economic insecurity, the decay of communities and the breakdown of families probably have had some impact on death and illness rates, in addition to the nation's opioid epidemic..."

This phenomena is exclusively due to psychological and social factors, and has nothing to do with physical illnesses, such as cancer, HIV, etc. I would call it a psychological side affect of the trends in affluent societies. There is ever increasing mental load on population, which has diminishing capacity to withstand it. Since the very childhood people live with the idea that money is the primary measure of success in life. But as with any talent, it is obviously not for everyone. There are other values of a human being, such as moral, or other talents, which seldom bring financial success, but they are largely neglected by most.

The farther we are from the roots of community and social structures, developed since the dawn of humanity, the more we prone to mental illness and, as a consequence, to physical decay.

This is not the full list of trends and their associated impacts on humanity. But statistics demonstrates without a trace of doubt that enormous forces of degradation march in parallel with technological and social progress.

All above-mentioned trends raise theoretical questions: are they inseparable companions of technological and social progress, or it is something in our power to stop or reverse these trends for betterment of advanced societies? If not, what their affect on a society could be in the distant future?

In this respect it is demonstrative to recall experiments of John Calhoun, who studied affect of different conditions on behaviour of social animals. The most famous one was conducted in 1968. Calhoun set up a "Utopian universe" for mice – a limited space where food, drink and other necessities were provided. There were no predators, no conceivable dangers for life. The experiment started with just 4 pairs of mice.

The population doubled every 55 days. It reached maximum 600 mice. As stated in Wikipedia, "This period between day 315 and day 600 saw a breakdown in social structure and in normal social behavior." The changes were drastic and profound: aggression, absence of interest in breeding, and others. Reproduction stopped completely. Homosexuality and violence, in spite of food abundance, were rampant. The mice population moved rapidly to its extinction. On the 1780 day of experiment the last member of this community died. The mice paradise ceased to exist.

In this experiment the limit of space was just a temporary factor. The more mice population died, the more space became available for the living. However, the behavior of society, once changed, had never reversed back to the "normal" mouse pattern. As Wikipedia put it, "…behavior patterns were permanently changed."

We can easily detect similar trends in the contemporary affluent societies. They all lead to one outcome: shrinking population.

Aftermath of shrinking population

The first consequence of shrinking population is easy to deduce: collapse of construction industry. There will be plenty of space from the previous generations, which will cost virtually nothing. The only expense will be maintenance. The world will live, the first time in human history, with huge oversupply of the living space, available for everyone.

Small cities will be abandoned, as few or any jobs will be available or needed. It would be expensive, and actually not economical, to demolish them, and they will be exposed to natural decay. There are already cities and villages like these in Russia, Italy, and some other countries.

In the suburbs, the first buildings to be abandoned will be the tallest ones. As soon as tenants start leaving them, the maintenance cost will spread among diminishing occupancy, which will force the remaining tenants to leave faster. As living space won't be a problem in big cities, the process will accelerate.

Collapse of construction industry will bring about many other far-reaching consequences. Industries supporting construction will collapse as well. Production of construction materials, construction machinery, communication, research and development, and related services will shrink accordingly. As population will be diminishing, the need for furniture and household items will also shrink to the level close to the maintenance of the existing items, or to the needs of their replacement.

As the productivity and living standard will be high, there will be no incentive to conduct research and development, or further increase productivity.

Apparently, fewer young people will be interested in obtaining college or higher education, as career won't give much advantage over those who are not on the same education level.

There will be more people who do not work, than in any previous period of the human history. This will be not only because the scarcity of jobs. The main reason will be that people will not want to work. This is actually an obvious contemporary trend in the developed world. According to Time magazine, "Nearly 40% of people in the United States aged 16 to 24 say that they don't want a job, accounting for a sizable portion of the 92 million Americans who are currently outside the labour force.." The number is 36.8 million! Just compare this mood to China, where any job is considered a great luck!

In all likelihood, because a widespread mental illness and lack of economic stimulus for work, the work force will shrink to the level insufficient to maintain the living standard achieved by previous generations.

With such great proportion of mentally ill and unemployed people it is reasonable to suggest that violent crimes will proliferate. With it, law enforcement industry will grow accordingly.

The socio-economic statistics reflects the overall trend of the human race: it is getting older as a biological organism. This aging has nothing to do with an average age of humans at any particular moment. This aging relates to humanity as a nature species, which has gone through its young years, maturity, and is about to enter the stage of decay. It will direct its mind towards further improving its living conditions, whereby accelerating its own degeneration. At this time it is impossible to predict all debilitating changes awaiting humanity. But for sure they will come: the more natural threats of survival we remove from our lives, the more unpredictable consequences we will have to deal with.

Our civilization has removed from its existence its main condition: survival of the fittest. Now we, as a society, are responsible for wellbeing of everyone, including those who have no ability, or no will or no desire to work hard to survive. This became a fertile ground for the seeds of degeneration and decay.

International Affairs in the Shrinking World

Since the dawn of humanity, acquisition of new territories was an important incentive for countries whose economy and military power gathered strength. It meant additional natural resources, exploitation of indigenous population, and wealth for the conqueror. In the not-so-distant future, it will no linger be an incentive. With shrinking population more territory will become vacant and of no use.

For almost every country, solar, wind and other sources of energy will be sufficient for providing energy needs. Conquering other territories and societies will become an obsolete idea from the economic point of view. The disputed territories – a painful issue in the contemporary relations among some countries – will cease to be the potential cause of military confrontation.

International economy dependencies, which began in the era of 'Globalisation', will expand even more. Even now, any disruption in moving goods and services in the contemporary international life could bring about serous hardships in affected countries.

However, there will always be countries like Russia, whose strive for acquisition of territories has nothing to do with the consideration of economy or wealth. It is just their way to ensure their dominance, to establish themselves as a great nation, without achieving prosperity and social progress to prove it. Russia is just an example: most likely this nation, for different reasons, will deteriorate even faster than the rest of the world.

Such countries will try to establish their dominance disregarding expediency and reasons of economical prosperity. The military potential of these countries will be significant. Should we expect a strong will of more peaceful countries to resist an assault?

Considering psychological decay of the most advanced nations, it is highly unlikely.

The will of the Western World to fight back and defend its value was weakening after WWI. A strong pacifistic mood spread over Western societies. Because of it, Western European countries made one concession after another to Hitler's demands, until the disaster, even greater than WWI, had struck: WWII.

After WWII, the pacifist ideas spread over developed world in the form of 'Peace Movement'. Its dominant thought was an unconditional surrender to communist assault in order to prevent nuclear holocaust. At that time the world already knew too well what communists would do if they come to power: mass terror and suppression of freedom, to name a few.

At present, a serious war against the developed world seems too remote a possibility. Its war technology arsenal is too big a deterrent to anyone. It ensures the long lasting peace for Western civilization. The longer the time of peace, the weaker the will of population and politicians to resist and fight will get. This is the low of nature: if something is not used, it will succumb to decay and atrophy.

Chapter 15. Impact of Robotics

Robot supposed to be a machine possessing some capability of a human brain, and perform limited, albeit complex, activity even in unpredictable circumstances. In sci-fi movies, picture books and illustrations a robot looks like a human made of metal or plastic parts, moving, speaking and doing "human" things. But so far, no true robot has been made. What available is a machine, or a group of machines, which act in the mode of certainty. There could be a large number of conditions, or combinations thereof, but a robot's response is pre-determined. In unpredictable circumstance a human interference can help, but otherwise a robot is just a different level of automation. To create a robot for a specific task, a process is broken down into groups of routine operations. Each individual group requires its own pre-programmed robot. This activity could be very complex, but does not suggest any degree of uncertainty, or unforeseeable skills.

Yet, what robots do is already impressive: they work under no supervision in manufacturing, do some house work, and even penetrate into intellectual sphere as artificial intelligence software. As of 2015, there are 66 robots per 10,000 workers world wide. Some analysts predict that robots will sweep the labour market by 2040. This is debatable.

But there are no robots which can replace humans even in comparatively simple activities under unpredictable circumstances. Robot's intelligence is far behind from that of even primitive mammals. Thus, a computer, which can beat the world chess champion, could hardly match its capability with half-brain of a rat.

The future of robotics is not only in the great number of independent units. It is already quite evident that a higher level of intelligence and management will be required. It will be just a matter of integrating largely available elements by artificial intelligence, afforded by powerful computers and software.

Consider, for example, individual transportation. There are already systems – call it robots – in place, that can drive a car automatically, without the driver's interference. There is a navigation system in place to guide the robot to the destination point. Cars already can park automatically with remarkable precision. There are systems allowing operating a car remotely: an owner can give the robot a command to leave the parking and roll to the place of the owner's choice. What remains to develop is a global system, which will gather the last-moment information on weather, road condition, traffic situation, individual's business or private schedule, and other data to fully automate the individual's transportation. Even more useful such a system will be for industrial and commercial use, which will include loading and unloading trucks, driving them to the point of destination and back, scheduling maintenance and repairs, and other functions.

In manufacturing, there are also many individual systems in place, just waiting for integration. There are fully automated stock management systems, employing robots and computers: no human interferes in its operation. Such a system is in operation at Amazon, and it makes no errors, and works faster and more efficient than humans.

There are robots in manufacturing facilities, working in assembly lines, in stock rooms, and other places. In order to organize a truly integrated production process, the higher intelligence mode has to gather on-line sales and customer order data from all retail-wholesale outlets, analyse it and send it to a manufacturer's brain center: if and when the decision is made to produce more of any product, the higher intelligence will give directives to purchasing departments to buy necessary materials, schedule production in the most efficient way, and give commands to robots to do the job. Other robots, working in the stock room, in maintenance department, transportation and financial areas will be coordinated and controlled accordingly.

In the recent past, medical diagnostics was exclusively the area of a medical expert. Now, most serious diagnostic is done by machines, although supervised by humans.

Some surgical operations are already performed by robots: their work is more accurate and reliable than that of humans.

There are miniature devices that can be attached to a human body: they can gather instantaneous information on all functions, and transmit it to the central higher-intelligence computer. In the outgoing patient rooms, there are monitors, which control all body functions and transmit this information to the central nurse's station. It will take a higher intelligence to integrate these activities: schedule an ambulance to pick up the patient, deliver him/her to the hospital, make final diagnostic by stationary machine, interpret results, deliver the patient to the operating room if necessary, and monitor recovery thereafter.

No doubt that thousands of military robots will be in place, doing the most dangerous jobs: they will be better than humans in detecting the enemy, and in eliminating them with deadly precision and efficiency. Some of such robots are already in operation, and it is only a matter of time to perfect them and put in service under command of higher intelligence.

Advancements in social and intellectual spheres will surpass all fantasies of the past generations. Google already started projects whose goal is to store in computer memory all printed data, which has ever been produced in the past history of humanity, and make it the basis for the higher intelligence analytics. Thus, all data about any individual on earth will be available and updated on-line: patterns of his/her behaviour will be analysed, and conclusions about an individual's behaviour will be drawn in accuracy not imaginable so far. Analysis of social trends, economy dynamics forecasts, and other intellectual activities will be raised to the new level.

As it stands now, we are still far away from robots which are capable of replacing cheap labour in retail, care for elderly, and numerous jobs in service and production. To build such robots, a major break-through in science and technology is required, particularly in software development and creation of new materials. A computer brain, equal to a few super computers, needs to be squeezed into a small space. Superconductors and sensors, probably with biological material, must be part of construction. There are many other, sociological and behavioural concepts, which do not exist yet, which must be addressed.

However, robotics is advancing by leaps and bounds, and will likely become a full-fledged industry in the next 40-50 years. Its impact on social life will be more profound than any technology has made so far.

All previous technological advancements had some positive and negative impacts on the economy and social life. As a rule, increased productivity eliminated some jobs, but also created others: as statistics demonstrates, the number of lost jobs is usually offset by the number of new jobs, required for the new technology. Often though the number of well-paid jobs falls, but the number of poorly paid job rises, particularly so in service sector. With robotics and higher intelligence integration it will be different: the number of new jobs will be much, much less than the number of jobs lost. Particularly hard blow will be dealt on the segment of low-skilled, low-paid jobs.

There are countries which need robots sooner, whereas others would rather prefer to delay robotics' assault.

Countries, which need them sooner are industrial societies which have low fertility rate, high living standard and averse to immigration. The most representative example of that is Japan. From 1990 to 2015 its working-age population has declined 11 percent, and shrinking 1.5 percent every year (VOX) . Its unemployment rate has dropped to 3.5 percent. Shrinking work force and soaring elderly population make Japan's economy very unstable and prone to recession for otherwise insignificant factors. That's why Japan is one of the most advanced countries in the field of robotics and automation.

But in other developed countries – the U.S. and Europe among them - where immigration supposed to replenish the work force of the local population which has low fertility rate, robotics will bring about many insurmountable problems. First, it will wipe out hundreds of millions jobs. Robots, being machines, do not need life or disability insurance, neither any other social aspect of employment. The quality of their work will confirm to standards not achievable by humans. So, the human aspect of employment will be resolved for good where robots are employed.

The U.S. will have to close doors on immigration from Mexico. Robotics will also create an unemployment exceeding that in the great depression of 1929-1933. To prevent a social upheaval, the country would have to adopt a new welfare policy, and initiate projects to employ this work force, as it was done at the time of Great Depression. This crisis will last much longer than the Great Depression: probably a few generations, until low fertility rate takes its toll and decrease the total population. No doubt that such number of idle people will represent enormous social problem and challenges to the whole society.

Particularly devastating consequence of robotics will be felt in countries which provide cheap labour in the global scale, such as China. In 40 years from now it will still have a few hundred millions of unskilled workers. Demand for Chinese production will diminish, as local robots would do it better without expense of transportation and other overheads. Supporting them by welfare system in China is out of the question: the country would not have a proper infrastructure for such economy. One can only speculate what will happen when such amount of people are left without means to support their lives.

How proliferation of robotics will impact human life? Must likely, it would have a devastating affect on human mental and physical health. There are already tractable trends indicating that accelerated progress of technology and improvement in life conditions do mostly harm to the health of homo sapience. Now, with all its intellectual power, no one can harm human race, except humans. And they do so by creating comfortable conditions to paralyze the stimulus to fight and survive.

Chapter 16. Summary

The second half of the 20th century witnessed events, which character, force, timing and consequences had stunned the best social and political science gurus. That's what happened - in chronological order:

- Iranian clerical revolution in 1979. Its consequence was a massive radical Islam assault on the Western world, accompanied with international terrorism
- China economic and political reforms - started in 1979. They elevated China to the global political and military power
- Disintegration of the former Soviet Union in 1991. This ended the Cold War and gave independence to all countries and satellites of the Soviet empire, along with decreasing influence of the U.S. on its alliances.

Surprising and impressive as these events had been, in retrospect they did not come out of the blue. They were consequences of social, economical and technological processes inside these societies, a logical outcome of hidden forces, which became evident and explainable only post-factum.

However important, such events are only elements in the chain of global trends, which are, in most part, not under control of decision-makers. Some trends are comparatively short, lasting just about a century; others may stretch a millennium or longer.

In the twentieth, and more so in the twenty-first century, social dynamics accelerated: long-lasting trends shrunk to decades; what in the past took a few centuries now lasts a hundred years or less. Statistics reflecting technology progress, as well as social, economic and demographic dynamics proof it with utmost clarity.

When circumstances change, decisions of affected governments are unpredictable, and oftentimes irrational, based on greed, suspicion, fear and ego. But the long-term trends create conditions for both rational, and irrational decisions, the consequences of which may last significant stretch of time.

The most visible trend affecting contemporary social life is technological progress. Its speed accelerated after the end of WWII, and since then its velocity shows no sign of abating. Along with it grows consumption of energy. No surprise that the remaining deposits of fossil fuels decrease at alarming rate. Oil supply particularly became of great importance to the global economy because of its use for transportation. It potentially could become the trigger of military conflicts of scale which might surpass all previous wars.

As oil reserves dwindle, a frantic search for alternatives intensified. Significant effort is directed towards developing alternative energy sources: Wind, solar, hydro and nuclear. Most promising of all – and environmental friendly – are wind and solar energy. Also an intensive research is under way in the field of fuel cell technology. It replaces combustion process, which theoretical efficiency limit is around 42 percent, with chemical process, with its theoretical efficiency ceiling of about 95 percent.

In the recent past oil has become the cause of international tensions and political games. Its impact on economies is understandable: when demand for oil rises, so does its price. When the price of oil rises, economies are affected in a negative way. This pattern changed in 2014: the world economy was improving, thereby increasing the demand for energy, but the oil price per barrel dropped from almost $140 in 2008 to below $50. This defies the logic of business activity relations, which supposed to be the opposite: the greater demand for energy, the higher is the price of oil. But as multiple sources indicate, the price of oil was changing in parallel with diminishing demand for it. This was attributed to a few dominant factors:

- Intensified shale oil extraction in the U.S.
- Production of biofuels
- Development of solar energy technology
- Development of wind energy technology

Solar and wind energy are renewables, a gift of nature, so to speak: it is a component of the earth's eco system. Once infrastructure of its capture is in place, the source is free for all, abundant, and clean. Obviously – within certain limits though – no harm to the environment.

Available solar energy potential is approximately 6,000 times greater than all sources of energy currently in use by humanity. However, its use for electricity production is often problematic: it is not spread evenly around the globe, and so is during the course of a day, or a season, and also depends on weather conditions. It needs supplementary energy sources or grid to alleviate gyrations of solar electricity generation.

Therefore, further expansion of solar technology depends on development and implementation of large energy storage infrastructure. There are a few options currently in use. One is construction of dams, into which water will be pumped when excessive solar electricity is generated. When electricity production is low and not sufficient, the hydro energy will be used to provide for the difference in supply and demand.

Where grid is close to solar power station, it can absorb the excessive electricity.

There are also a few new technologies under development, the most promising of which is development of powerful electric batteries, capable of storing large amount of energy at low cost.

Nonetheless, solar energy technology progress is impressive. In 1950, the price per watt of installed capacity was $300. In 2015 it was about $0.30, which is about 1,000 times less. It is expected to reach $0.03 kWt/hr in the next few years.

Efficiency of PV solar batteries in production so far was just 15%. Recently, panels with efficiency of about 25% were in use. Laboratory efficiency of some panels now is 46 percent, but most advanced laboratories achieved the efficiency of 95 percent.

Our calculations demonstrate that by 2030 solar energy capacity, in the imaginary best case scenario, will reach 32 percent of generated electricity (not to mistake for total energy demand).

Wind electricity generation is the fastest growing renewable energy technology. As its source is also free, the cost of its electricity is predictable for many years into the future. Therefore long-term contract could be signed with such an enterprise.

Wind technology has similar problems of energy storage as the solar one. For the wind turbine to be effective, the wind speed must be between 7 and 17 meters per second. If the wind is less, almost no electricity is generated. With the speed faster than this range, the turbine must be shut down to prevent its destruction. For good measure, a wind farm often far away from consumers, therefore costly transmission infrastructure should be build. These, and other issues of technological and environmental nature must be resolved to make this technology work at its maximum efficiency and sufficiently cost-effective. However, with all this, according to Wind Energy Foundation, it's cost now is "...averaged just 4 cents per kilowatt hour, which is 50% lower than in 2009".

In the year 2000 the world wind power capacity was 17,400 MW. In 2014 it was 369,553 MW: in 14 years it grew 2,100 percent.

The leader of this technology is China, but the U.S. and Western Europe is not far behind.

The total potential of wind power on Earth is 1,000 terawatts. In 2012 the total energy human consumption was about 20 terawatts. The saturated point, when the further wind energy extraction will harm the environment is 250 terawatts, which is a long way to go.

A significant incentive in wind and solar energy investment is instability of fossil fuel supply, limited and depleting fossil fuel reserves, and harmful affect of combustion process on the environment.

As benefits of solar and wind technologies are so obvious, would it be unrealistic to suggest that the whole world unanimously decided to invest in these technologies sufficient funds to produce from them 100% of electricity, replacing all fossil fuel power facilities?

According to our calculation, solar and wind generated electricity should reach in 2030 19,391 TWh, of which wind generated electricity would be 13,497 TWh, and solar generated electricity 5,471 TWh. To achieve this, the world should invest close to $10 trillions in wind, and about $5.4 trillions in in solar energy, assuming that in a few years from the time of this writing the efficiency of solar panels will reach 46%.

Thus, total investment in these technologies must be approximately $15.4 trillions in 17 years (starting from 2013), or about $905 billions each year during this period – an astronomical, unrealistic amount under contemporary circumstances.

If investment amount will be the same as in the last few years - $80 billion in wind, and $112 billion in solar technology - it would take 124 years for wind, and 49 years for solar to reach the electricity demand projected for 2030.

Electricity is only a part of total energy consumption. There is huge, and ever increasing demand for energy by transportation. It goes in parallel with ever-shrinking oil reserves and flat conventional oil production. There is a clear evidence that the dynamics of oil production confirms Peak Oil Theory, which is dated back to the beginning of twentieth century. According to it, a plateau of oil production will be reached at some time in the future, after which it will decline no matter how many new discoveries would me made. Now its validity is quite clear. It is a widely acknowledged notion among geologists that more than 95 percent of all discoverable conventional oil has now been found. New discoveries are labour intensive. The best numerical evidence of it is EROEI – Energy Returned On Energy Invested. A hundred years ago it took one barrel of oil to produce 100 barrels of oil. In 2010, one barrel of oil spent produced just 9 barrels of oil used. New reserves of conventional oil have even lesser yield: one barrel of oil spent produce only 5 barrels of oil used. Shale oil is even worse, having EROEI just 4:1.

Now the evidence is that conventional oil production reached its plateau in 2008, and stays around 72-75 million barrels a day. An optimistic forecast is that after 2020 its production will enter the phase of steady decline.

Under such condition oil price should have risen to new heights. Instead, reaching almost $140 per barrel, the price of oil dropped sharply in 2014 to below $50 per barrel. The reason for it is the increase of shale oil production in the U.S. It offsets the increase for international oil demand by almost 100 percent.

However, with expected increase of oil demand by more than 20 million barrels a day after 2020, American shale oil production will no longer be sufficient to fill-up the gap. Shale oil production has already reached its plateau in the U.S., and no effort would increase its production.

Proliferation of shale oil production to other countries is a very unlikely scenario. Only America has an expertise and technology to extract shale oil. Between 2000 and 2010 a total of 17,268 exploratory gas wells were drilled in the US, as compared to about 50 wells drilled in the EU.

The weighted average of shale oil production cost is approximately $60 per barrel. Considering environmental damage it would eventually amount to $80 per barrel. It is therefore reasonable to assume that until 2020 the price of oil will not rise above $80 per barrel. However, when then shale oil production will not be enough to fill the gap between supply and demand, the oil price should skyrocket.

This situation may change if advancement in fuel cell technology would be fast enough to reach its theoretical efficiency level of 70-95 percent in the 2020s. Then it would profoundly affect oil prices, and prolong the life of existing conventional oil reserves for more than 50 years.

Fuel cell cost dynamics is impressive: in 2002 a cost of 1 kW of fuel cell produced electricity was $275. In 2012 it was $47 per 1 kW, and in 2017 it is expected to be $30 per kW.

If fuel cell technology is a success then, taking into account an ever-increasing energy demand for transportation, conventional oil production will stay at the existing plateau of around 72-75 million barrels a day. The price of oil will still rise, likely to be about $80 per barrel or higher by 2030, but no major disaster will be looming in terns of oil shortage.

If fuel cell technology is not up to its optimum cost efficiency, the energy crises is imminent. Shale oil production will no longer be a factor after 2020. In 2020-2025 increased demand for oil will push its price to $200 per barrel or higher. By 2030, as calculations in this work suggests, the price of conventional oil per barrel would reach about $600 per barrel. This means that a car trip of 100 km. (64 miles) would use about $960 of gasoline. A return flight ticket Toronto-Paris in economy class would cost about $6,500.

In general, the consequences are:

- End of suburban life as we know it in North America and, to a lesser extent, in Western Europe. Suburban life is supported only by the use of private cars. As the price of gasoline becomes beyond the means of middle class, people will have to move to the cities, closer to the place of employment, where a car will be used much less, or not at all.
- A car will become an ultimate luxury item. The auto industry will shrink likely by 70-80 percent. Demise of the auto industry will cause massive unemployment, as there are many other industries which depend on the auto industry.

- Road building and maintenance will also shrink, along with the new suburban construction and maintenance. This will exacerbate unemployment further.
- The car fleet over the world will shrink by about 80 percent
- Sharp increase in prices of agricultural products, as most fertilizers are manufactured from petroleum derivatives. This will end food subsidies, food banks and food stamps, and all free niceties, invented by our society. As a large part of developed world population depends on government subsistence, the outcome is predictable: unrest and massive criminal activity.

A host of other consequences are expected: suburban defaults, mass unemployment, unprecedented financial crisis, collapse of medical services around the globe, etc.

International affairs will no longer be regulated by the UN decisions, and more so by its principles. A further fragmentation of Middle East countries, composed with different ethnic groups, should be expected.

Oil prices below $70-$80 per barrel will likely last until 2020. The majority of oil producing countries need a fiscal budget break-even price greater than $100 per barrel. As they have no infrastructure to support their life by other industries, they are heading into severe hardships, turmoil and possibly disintegration.

The Muslim world is deeply divided by sectarian hatred between Shia and Sunni. This stand-off is centuries old, and there is no chance of reconciliation in foreseeable future. Therefore, Middle East major oil exporting countries will continue supporting sectarian fights, as well as international terrorism.

A peculiar feature of radical Islam is its hatred of the Western civilization, in spite of the fact that the Western world is tolerant to it more than common sense suggests. Muslim clerics though say little about Oriental powers, notably China and Japan, although these countries have no tolerance to the Muslim faith, and prohibit Muslim immigration.

There is anther deeply rooted cause of coming unrest and fights in the Middle East countries: their ethnical diversity. Table 18 shows ethnical composition of major countries in this region. In the past, these countries had been empires. Their disintegration started centuries ago, and so far has not been completed yet. The process is fuelled by interference of major global powers due to concern about terrorism and safety of oil supply. History of all empires proofs that ethnical fights never stop until independence of large ethnical groups is achieved.

Iran social stability is threatened by Kurds. As soon as their state is established on the ruins of Iraq and Syria, Iranian and Turkish Kurds will try to join their people, with whom they have a commonality of territory, language, culture and customs.

Azeri is another problem for Iran. They have a common border with Azerbaijan, the country with homogeneous Azeri population. Without Iranian border they would have a common geography, language, and culture.

Peace process between Arabs and Jews is the greatest hoax of the modern time. Israel is the land of dispute. Arabs claim that this land is theirs. Jews claim that this is the biblical land of Jews. Whether Jews are right or wrong, it matters nothing: they have nowhere to go, and therefore have no choice but to fight for their survival.

This problem can not be settled between countries which are at different stages of civilization. Spiritual and religious differences between Muslims and Jews are enormous. International support for Palestinians adds fuel to the flame. These are the foundation of the peace process.

If not for spiritual anti-Jewish sentiments in the Christian world, and its dependency on Arab oil, the conflict between Palestinians and Israel would look tiny in comparison with other conflicts around the globe. American, Russian and European countries involvement in the 'peace process' only complicate this issue.

The future of Russia is definitely not bright. Russia is also a remnant of an empire, whose deterioration became obvious long before the collapse of the Soviet Union. This process is irreversible for a number of reasons, and likely be completed when Russia would have neither funds, no population to supports its army, police and vital social institutions.

Russian policy is deeply rooted in its history. Its primary features are military expansion and oppression of population. After a short period of chaos in 1990s the situation stabilized and Russia resumed its expansion: war with Georgia and Ukraine, annexation of Crimea, Chechnya and Abkhazia, and preparation for further moves towards their Western neighbors is just the beginning. Brainwashing of population intensified. Its success is rested on two millennium-long postulates: Russian nation is superior over all others: Russia is surrounded by enemies, whose purpose is to conquer the Russian land and its riches.

In essence, Russian ruler's hostility towards America and Western Europe has the same cause as it was at the time of the Soviet Union: to divert attention of people from the country's inability to provide meaningful economic and social prosperity.

But since the government and the Russian majority formed a solid unity, it is reasonable to expect that this centuries-old policy will continue until such time when the whole economy will collapse, and the government will not be able to function. It may sound unrealistic to expect, but the first signs of it already show up.

The most convincing evidence of contemporary government financial abyss is its lease of some Siberian territory to China for the period of 49 years. Russia has always been obsessed with territories, but this is the sign of a major crack in its thinking at the Far East.

There are a few trends in this country, which accelerate in passing years:

- Flight of capital from Russia
- Constant emigration, most part of it is professionals with higher education
- High mortality rate, low fertility rate, and negative population growth
- Diminishing capital investment into industries
- Deterioration of the nation's physical and mental health

Besides, the country has numerous structural, political, and geographical problems, which have no solution.

The other reason for the Russian government aggressive stand is geopolitical considerations. Any such consideration is based on an assumption: *what if?*

So *what if* Western Europe indeed gets back to its aggressive stand and moves against Russia in an attempt to acquire its vast resources? *What if* Ukraine invites the US or NATO military force to its territory, which is a few hundred kilometres from Moscow? *What if* Turks decide to move north, to take over Caucasus? *What if* Iran decides to take over Azerbaijan? There are many *what ifs*. None of them, from geopolitical point of view, should be ignored, but not necessarily worked upon.

What if strategic thinking is not just the property of empires or strong states. It is also a component of smaller states' policy, whose existence depends on their affiliation with stronger states or blocks. Naturally, all Russian neighbours, who were under the dictatorship of the former Soviet Union, think the same way, but from different perspective: *what if* Russia moves in, to subjugate them again?

It seems that the Russian rulers are under delusions of such assumptions, and covey to its people as an established fact. To take the population back to reality Russia needs the change of power. But it is not possible, and not only because the unwillingness of the existing elite to lose it. There are reasons why Russia cannot adopt the path to restructuring and democracy: the most aggressive groups will use freedom to usurp the power, and abolish democracy.

The last chapter of the book is about the future of humanity in 100 years. Diminishing fertility rate per woman is the global trend. It is more pronounced in Western civilization, and also in the industrial societies of the Orient, the largest ones being China and Japan. The main cause is accelerated urbanization, but there are some others, examined in the book.

Calculations show that with the contemporary fertility rate Japan's population 100 years will be about 31 million. In the same period, the white race number will drop from 1 billion, as of the time of this writing, to 235 million.

In the past, the better was food supply, the more children a family could afford. Population growth though was accompanied by epidemics, which significantly reduced the population. This nature's mechanism was changed in 19th century: it was terminated due to progress in medicine, agriculture and industrial technologies.

Exponential population growth in the last 50-60 years is particularly remarkable. It was accompanied by reduced fertility rate, which seems as a paradox if compared with the previous demographic history and fundamentals. The explanation is, that life expectancy has increased, and so does the population whose age is beyond the boundary of fertility. This means that at certain point in time the number of people will drop. As calculation shows, the population, at a certain time, will be shrinking 50% every 25 years.

To demonstrate the point, a case of fictitious country, called Happy Planet Republic, was presented under assumption that its fertility rate is 1, a new generation is born every 25 years, and life expectancy is 75 years. According to calculation, the gerontological population growth there will last only 50 years. After this period the population shrinks 50 percent each 25 years.

In light of this a similar calculation of real situation is presented: a dynamics of Japan population. As Japan has no immigration, has aging population, and low fertility rate, it is ideal for calculation of its future demographics. According to this calculation, a hundred years from now Japan's population will shrink from 127 million to 31 million.

According to this methodology, calculation of white race demographics was presented, also using the factual data from 1 billion, as it is now, it would shrink to 235 millions.

There is a number of social, physiological, and behavioural pattern of societies, and factors, which influence such developments. The most prominent of them are:

162

- Ever increasing number of adult children live with their parents
- Growing number of single occupancy household
- Growing number of mentally ill
- Single parenthood
- Biological deterioration of human species

In many aspects the future of human species looks similar to the 'Utopian Universe' experiment of John Calhoun, who studied behaviour of social animals. He set up a cage for 4 mice, and provided them unlimited food and drink. After initial fast population growth mice behaviour changed in a profound way. Homosexuality, violence, and indifference to breeding was rampant. Mice population was shrinking, and after 1789 days from the beginning of the experiment the last member of the community died. The mice paradise ceased to exist.

Affect of shrinking population will be more profound than its growth. It will bring about the collapse of construction industry, automotive industry, shrinkage of social services, financial crisis and other consequences.

International affairs in the shrinking population world may take an unexpected twists. There will be no incentive to acquire new territories, or exploit other countries population. However, there always be countries like Russia or Iran, whose expansionist ambitions have nothing to do with economic consideration. Their success will depend on the will and determination of other countries to resist the aggression. Considering moral, physical and mental deterioration of population, consequences are unpredictable.

Appendix 1. Wind and Solar Energy Development in Numbers

The most essential data on energy generation and consumption is energy expressed in TWh (Terawatt per hour), which is the energy actually produced. Its statistics related to wind and solar PV energy from 2011 to 2013 is presented in the table 1.

Table A1-1. Electricity production in TWh – 2011-2013

Year	Wind TWh	Solar TWh	total
2011	446.4(**)	59.2(*)	505.6
2012	520(***)		
2012		94.1(*)	614.1
2013	683.0(*****)	140.6(****)	823.6

Sources:
* BP report
**
http://www.eia.gov/cfapps/ipdbproject/iedindex3.cfm?tid=6&pid=37&aid=12&cid=regions&syid=2007&eyid=2011&unit=BKWH
***
http://www.eia.gov/cfapps/ipdbproject/iedindex3.cfm?tid=6&pid=37&aid=12&cid=regions&syid=2007&eyid=2011&unit=BKWH
**** http://www.renewableenergyfocus.com/view/40266/
***** http://www.renewableenergyfocus.com/view/40266/

In terms of installed capacity, which produced this energy, its statistics is presented in the table A1-2. This table also contains capability of one GW (Gigawatt) of installed capacity to produce average amount of TWh energy by a particular technology.

Table A1-2. Wind and Solar installed and Generated Capacity.

Wind GW	Wind Generated TWh	Solar GW	Solar Generated TWh	Total TWh	TWh per 1 GW capacity - wind	TWh per 1 GW capacity -solar
283	520	100	94.1	614.1	1.84	0.94
315.7	683	134.7	140.6	823.6	2.16	1.04

To round up, in 2013:
- 1 GW of wind technology capacity generates 2 TWh electricity
- 1 GW solar technology capacity generates 1 TWh electricity

Below, the Table A1-3 contains the following (from previous calculations):

- Projected cumulated wind capacity in 2030
- Projected solar capacity in 2030
- Projected energy generated by wind capacity
- Projected energy generated by solar capacity

Table A1-3. Installed facilities production following in 2030:

Year	Wind cumulated capacity GW	Wind Generated TWh	Solar Capacity GW	Solar Generated TWh	Total TWh
2030	1480 (*)	3,889 (*)	1696 (**)	1696**	55,585

* Table 13. Wind power forecast, Chapter 4
** Table 8. Future of solar energy electricity, Chapter 3.

The ratio of wind/solar generated energy, is therefore 3,889/1,696 = 2.29

In 2012, electricity generation by fuel was as shown the table A1-4.

Table A1-4. Electricity generation by fuel, shown as percent in total. *

Year	Total TWh	Oil	Coal/Peat/ Shale	Natural gas	Hydro	Rene wable	Nucl.
2012	22,668	5	40.4	22.5	16.2	5	10.9

* IEA

Thus, fossil fuel generated 40.4 + 22.5 + 5 = 67.9% electricity. In terms of TWh it is 22,668 x 0.679 = 15,391.5 TWh.

Assuming demand growth 36 percent, as was forecasted by BP, the total electricity production in 2030 will reach 22,668 * 1.36 = 30,828 TWh.

If the ratio of fossil fuel generated electricity remains the same, it will produce in 2030 the following: 30,828 x 0.629 = 19,391 TWh.

Assuming that the wind/solar ratio will remain the same 2.29 in 2030 (see calculation above), to replace fossil fuel generated electricity by wind and solar, the wind must generate 13,497 TWh, the solar must generate 5,894 TWh.

Using the above calculated ratio between installed capacity and generated energy, Table A1-5 presents the calculated capacity.

Table A1-5. Required installed capacity of wind and solar by 2030

Total TWh	Wind TWh	Solar TWh	Wind capacity GW (2.6)*	Solar capacity GW (1)*
19,391	13,497	5,894	6,248	5,894

* 13,497/2.16 = 6,248. 5,894/1 = 5,894. see table A1-2.

Using these numbers we can calculate amount of wind capacity investment necessary to achieve this goal. According to GWEC report of 2012, in 2011, 40.6 GW was added, with the investment of USD $68 billion. This means that 1 GW of wind power cost $1.67 billion. In the previous presentation the calculated the cost of 1 GW of installed solar capacity was $0.95 billion.

Table A1-6 shows investment necessary to substitute fossil fuel by wind and solar generated electricity.

Table A1-6. Required investment to replace fossil generated electricity.

Technology	Installed	desired	To be added	Cost per GW bil.	Total investment bil	Investment bil. per year (17 years)
Wind	316	6,248	5,932	1.67	9,906	583
Solar PV	135	5,894	5,759	0.95	5,471	322
Total					15,377	905

This scenario, from the perspective of year 2015, is unrealistic. For comparison, in 2013 investment in wind was $80 billion, and investment in solar was $112 billion. The total annual investment must be $192 billion.

If investment level remains the same, the wind technology will reach this capacity in 9,906/80 = 124 years. For solar it will be 5,471/112= 49 years.

Reference

* REN21.net report
* https://en.wikipedia.org/wiki/Solar_energy#Potential (Ren.net report.)
* REN21. 2014. Renewables 2014 Global Status Report
*https://en.wikipedia.org/wiki/Solar_power
* IEA
* (http://www.renewable-energysources.com/)
*http://en.wikipedia.org/wiki/Cost_of_electricity_by_sour ce
*http://en.wikipedia.org/wiki/Solar_cell#Organic.2Fpoly mer_solar_cells
* Ren.21-net.pdf.
* REN21 Renewables 2014 Global Status Report
* REN21
* (Wind Enrgy Foundation, http://www.windenergyfoundation.org/about-wind-energy/economics)
* EWEA. (http://www.ewea.org/fileadmin/files/library/publications/reports/Economics_of_Wind_Energy.pdf)
* (Wind Energy Foundation).
* (Wikipedia, Petroleum Industry in China).
* (Ren21.net)
* (http://www.statista.com/statistics/307194/top-oil-consuming-sectors-worldwide/)
*http://www.energytrendsinsider.com/2014/07/10/world-sets-new-oil-production-and-consumption-records/
* (http://ostseis.anl.gov/guide/oilshale/)
* (GeoArabia, vol. 14, no 1, 2009. World Production of conventional petroleum liquids to 2030: A comparative overview, by Moujahed Al-Husseini).
* (Decline Curve Analysis of Shale Oil Production by Linnea Lund)
* (source: VOX report, Jan. 2015)

* (Wikipedia, Eagle Ford Formation.)
*http://www.hydrogen.energy.gov/pdfs/12020_fuel_cell_
system_cost_2012.pdf
* Www.sofcanada.com/index.php/primer
* http://www.eia.gov/tools/faqs/faq.cfm?id=41&t=6
* U.N. Projections
* The World Factbook
* (UN, World Urbanization Prospects.
* The World Book (31)
(http://www.washingtonpost.com/blogs/wonkblog/wp/201
4/12/18/the-unbelievable-rise-of-single-motherhood-in-
america-over-the-last-50-years/)
* Mark Z Jacobson, Atmosphere/Energy program,
Department of Civil Environmental Engineering, Stanford
University
* Solar FAQs
*http://www.peakprosperity.com/podcast/89793/shocking
-data-proving-shale-oil-massively-over-hyped